MODERN CLASSIC SONATAS

BOOK 3

Dr. Anis I. Milad

authorHOUSE®

AuthorHouse™
1663 Liberty Drive
Bloomington, IN 47403
www.authorhouse.com
Phone: 1 (800) 839-8640

"This book "Modern Classic Sonatas - Book 3 and Book 4" includes sonatas which were composed
by Dr. Anis I. Milad. Dr. Milad expressed his emotion and was able to complete each sonata in three
parts "exposition, development, and recapitulation" and in a variety of Key Signature. These sonatas
are also published in YouTube. Producing books to include this form of music is a door for the new
generations to follow and improve the classic music. This book is also produced to get the attention of
the conductors and the musicians around the world to our world in the United States of America"

Published by AuthorHouse 07/12/2019

ISBN: 978-1-7283-1876-9 (sc)
ISBN: 978-1-7283-1875-2 (e)

Print information available on the last page.

This book is printed on acid-free paper.

Contents

Score

Sonata No 21, Op 81 - The Sparrows and the Camphor Trees

Dr. Anis I. Milad

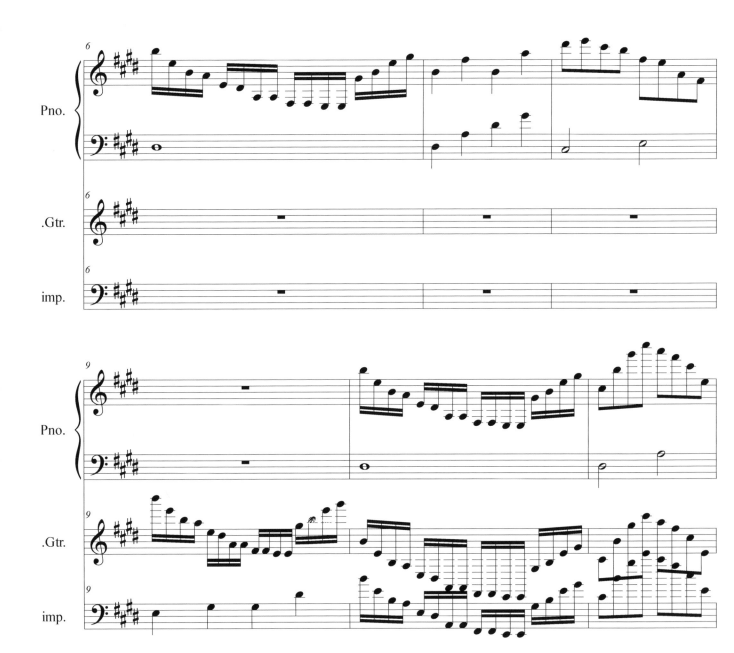

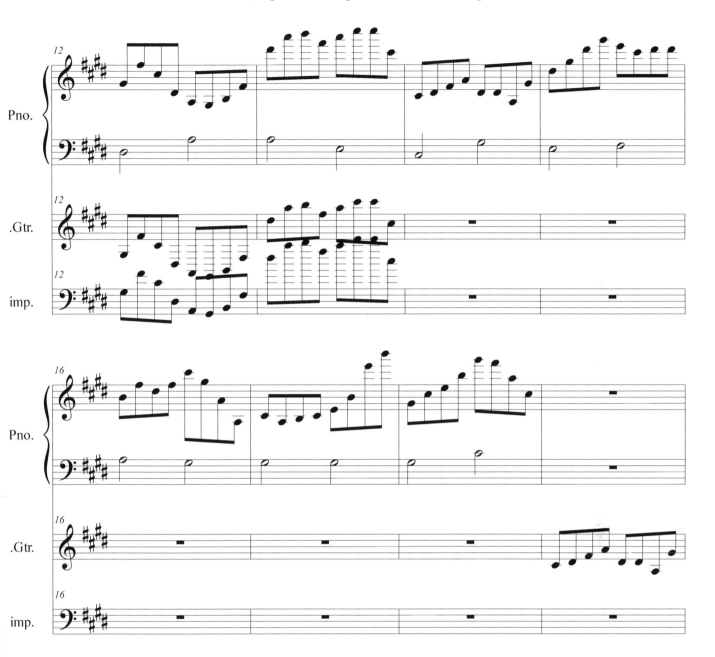

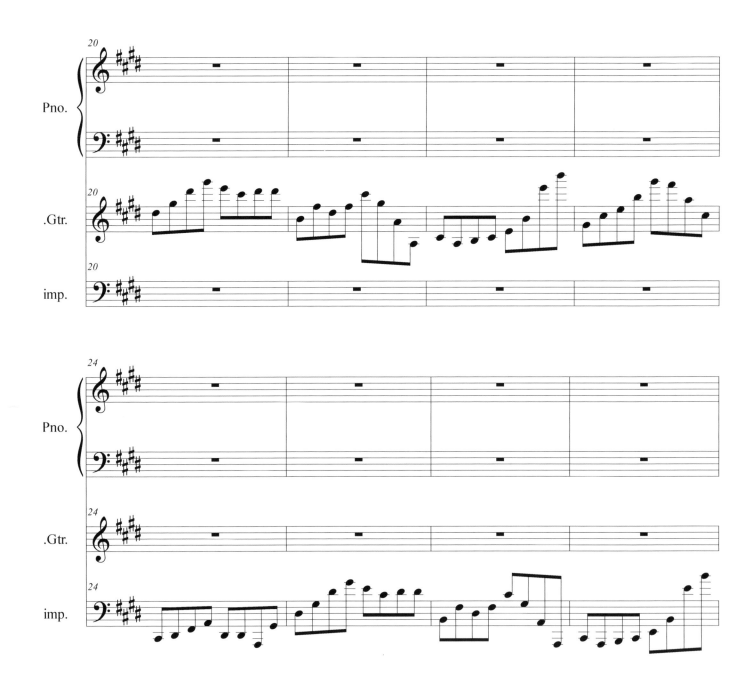

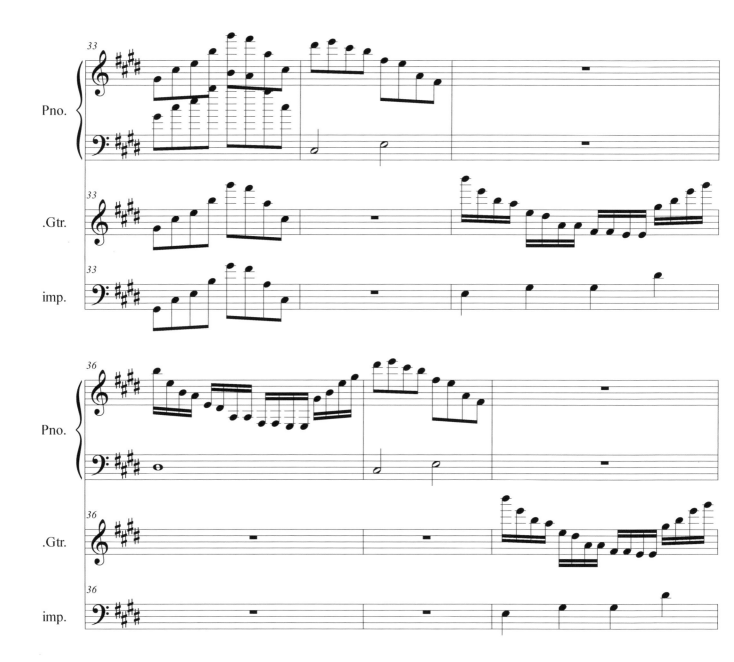

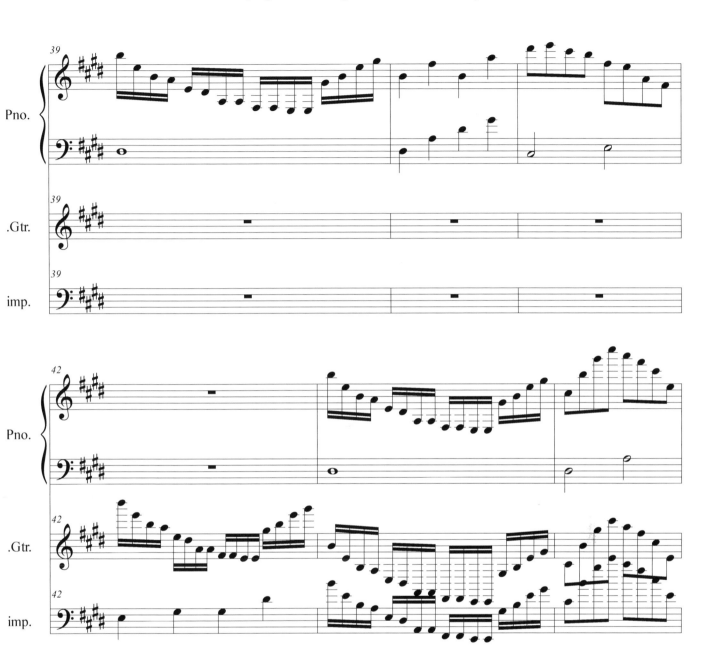

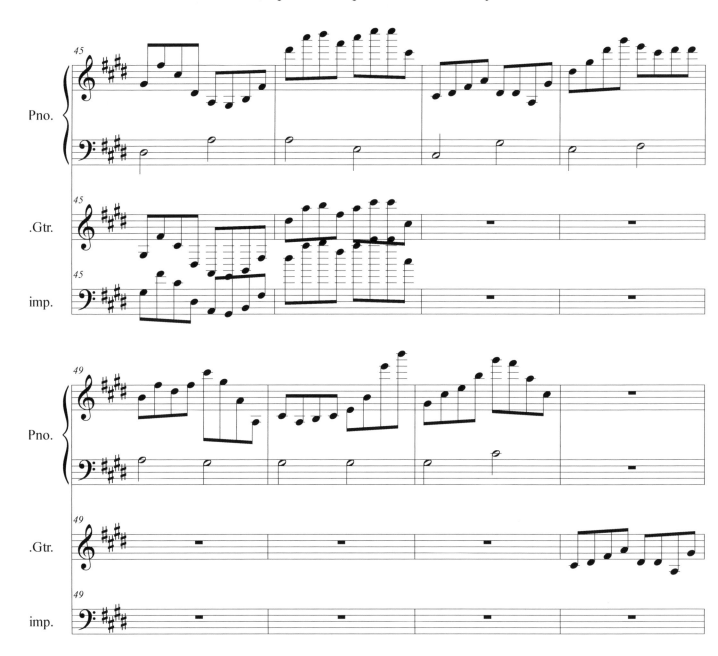

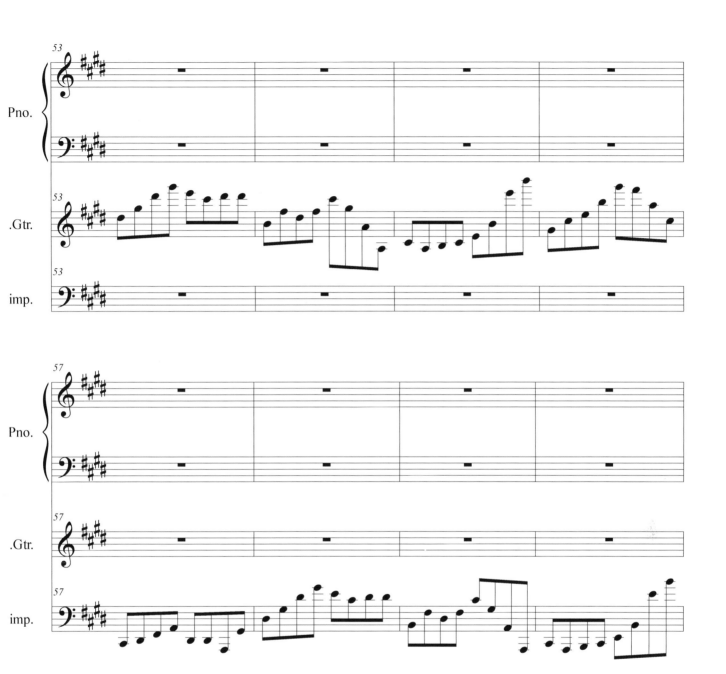

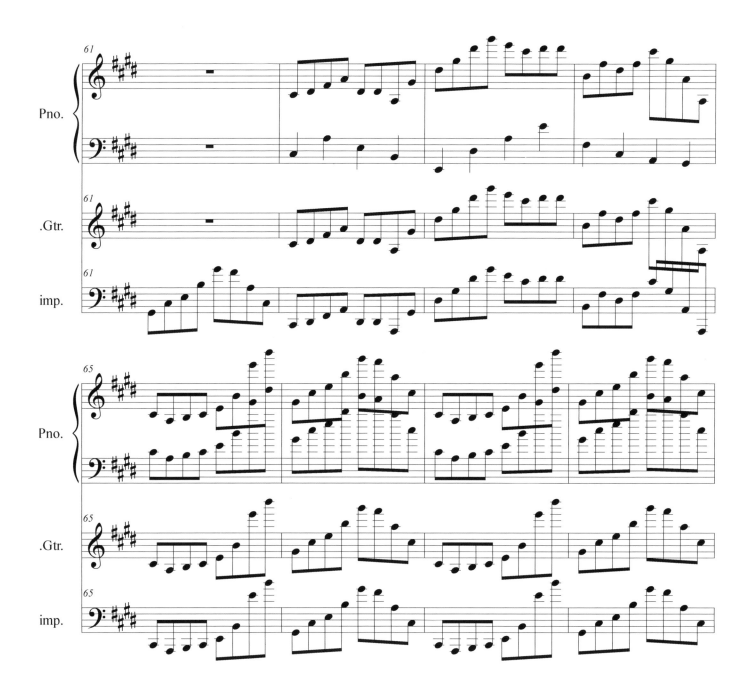

Sonata No 21, Op 81 - The Sparrows and the Camphor Trees

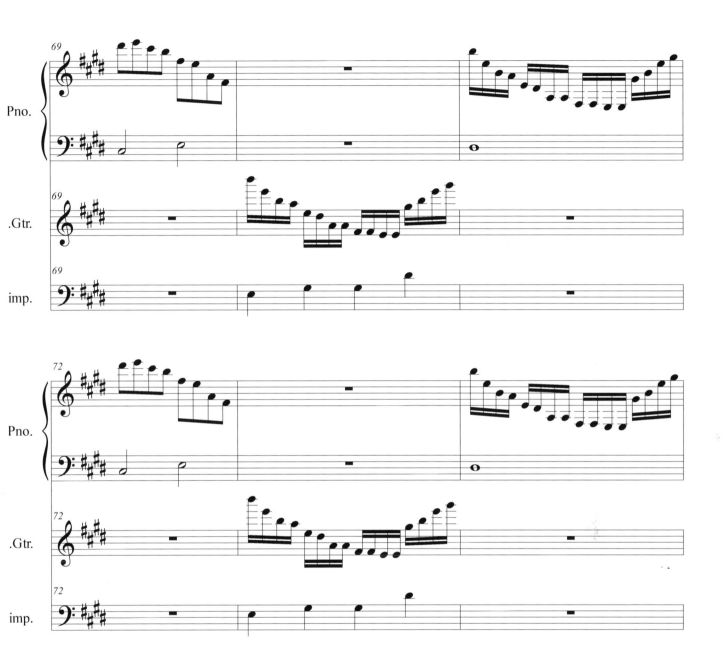

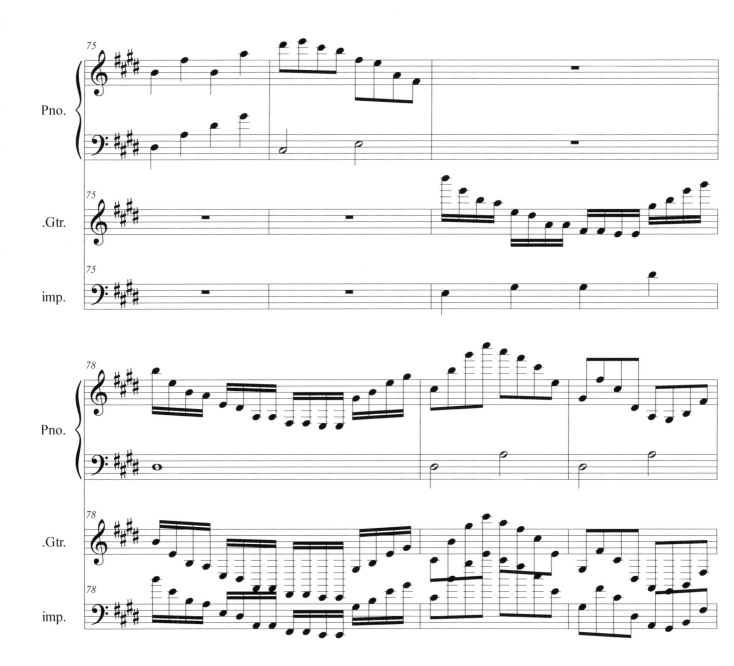

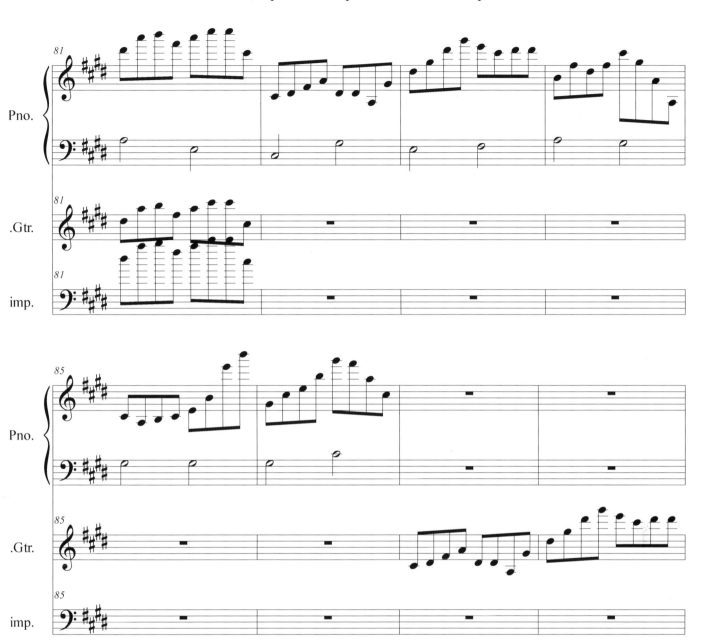

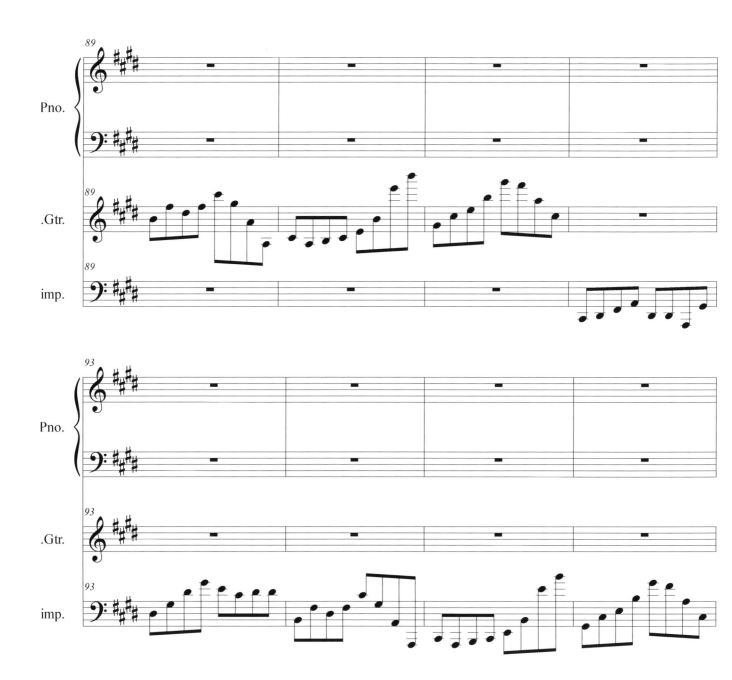

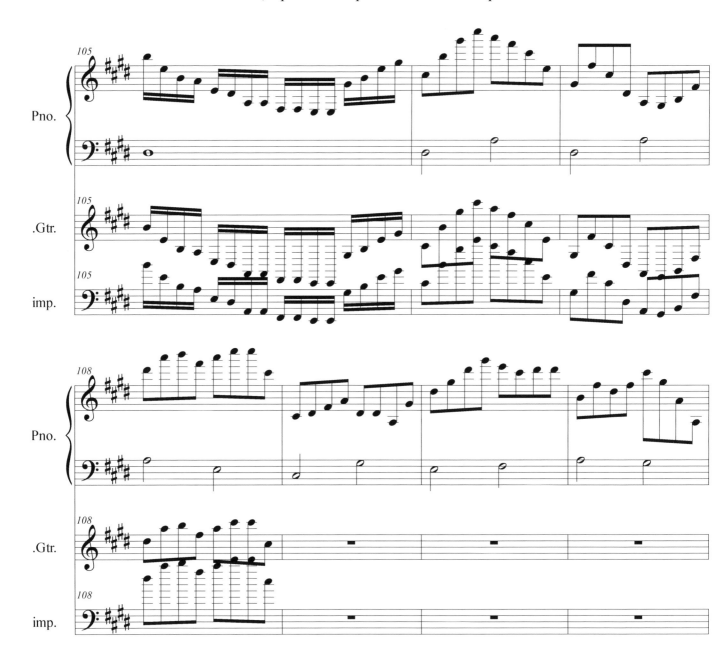

Sonata No 21, Op 81 - The Sparrows and the Camphor Trees

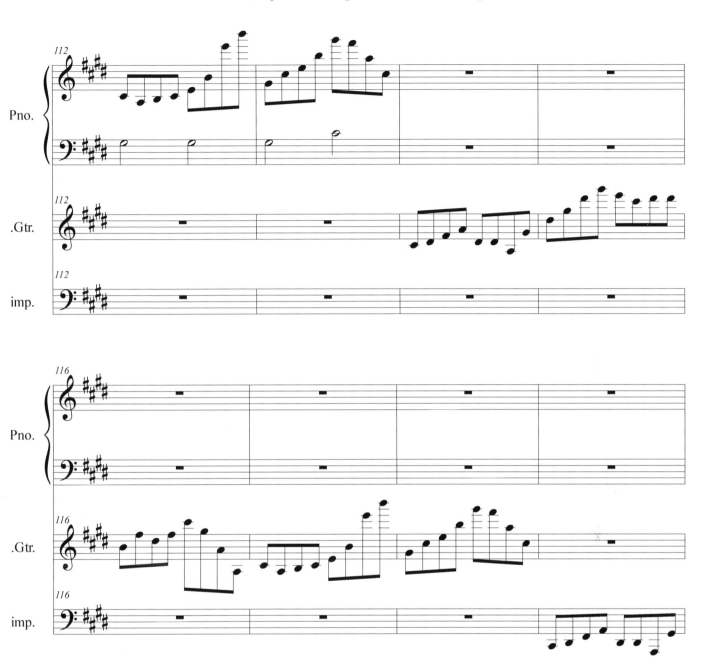

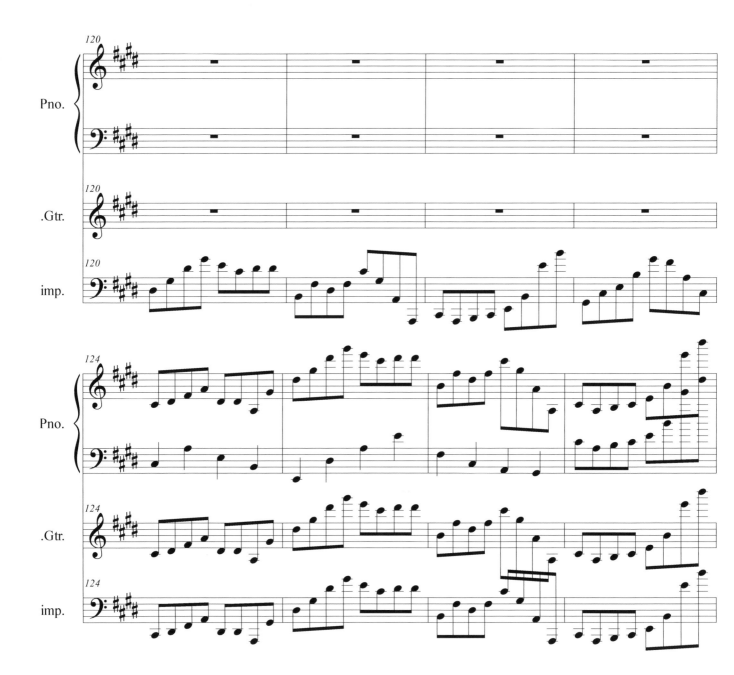

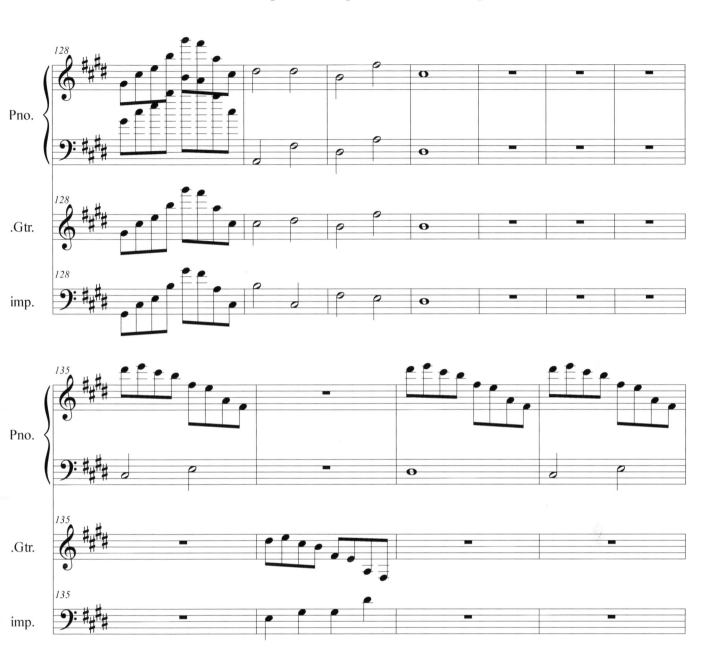

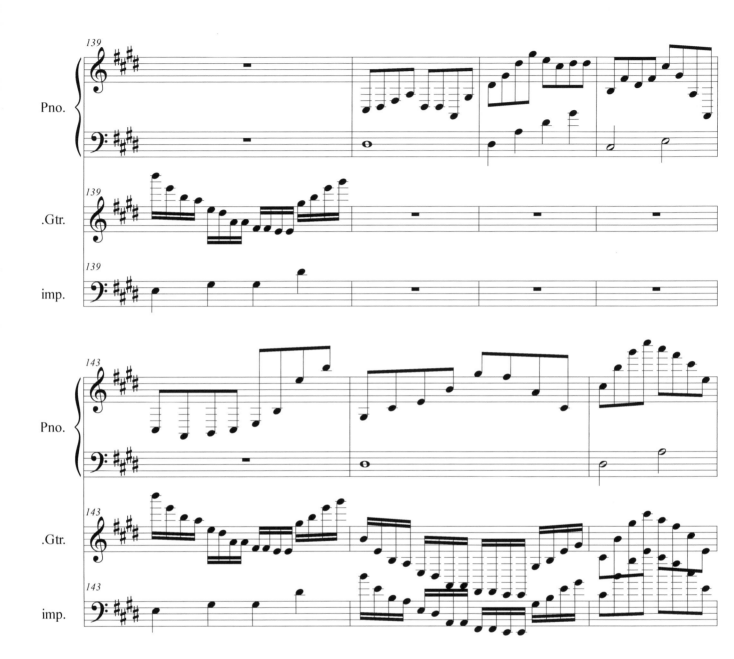

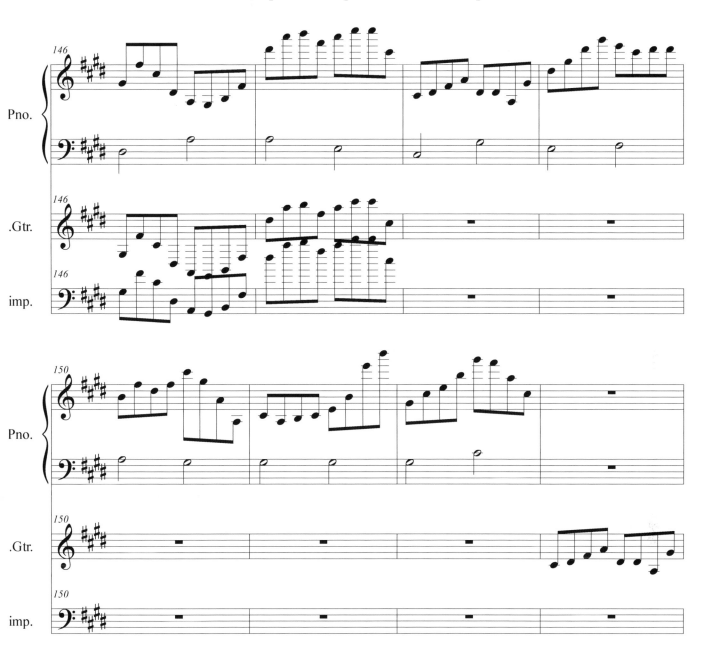

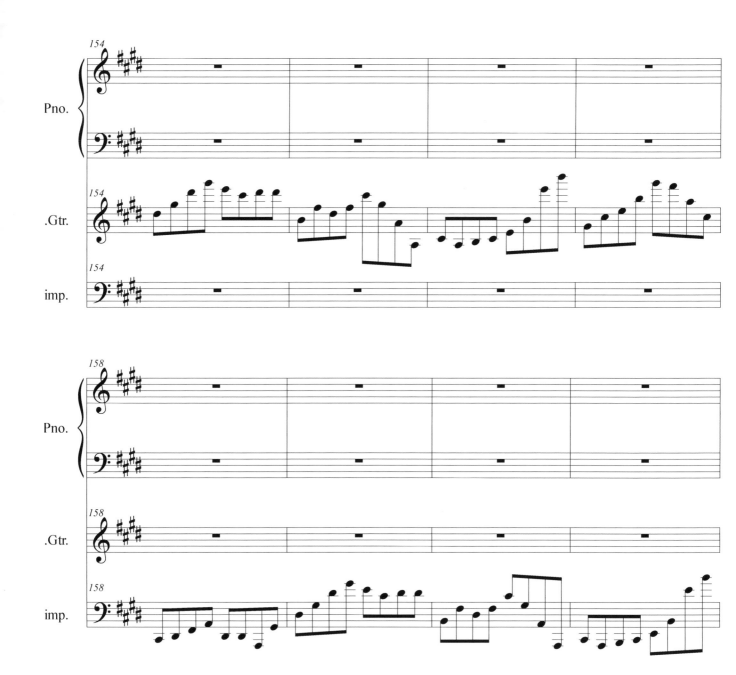

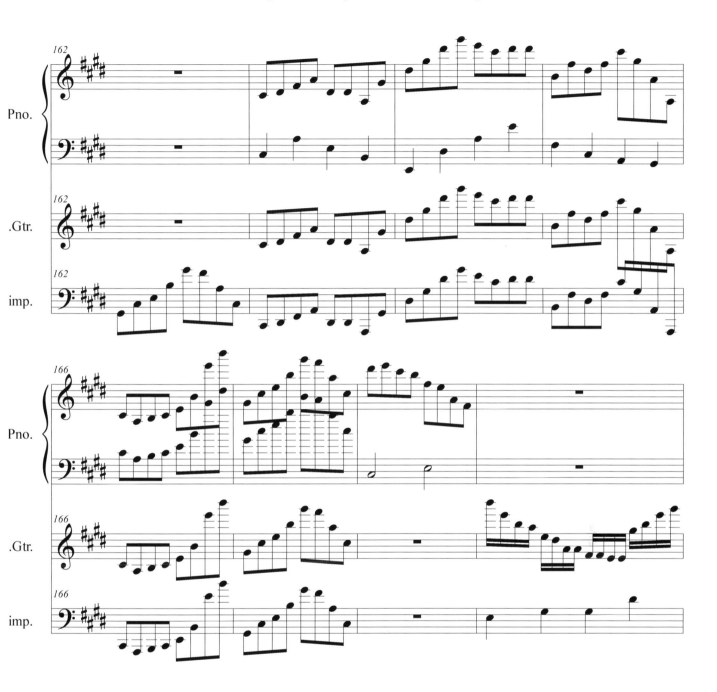

Sonata No 21, Op 81 - The Sparrows and the Camphor Trees

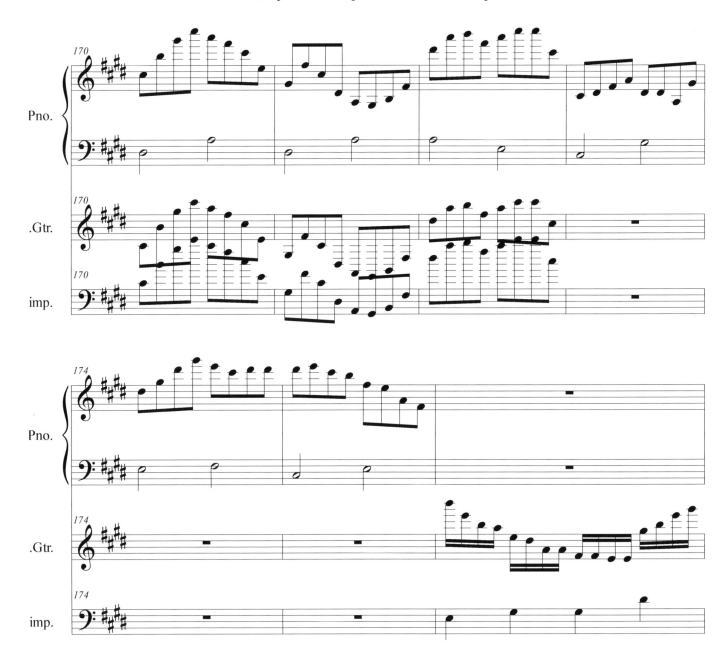

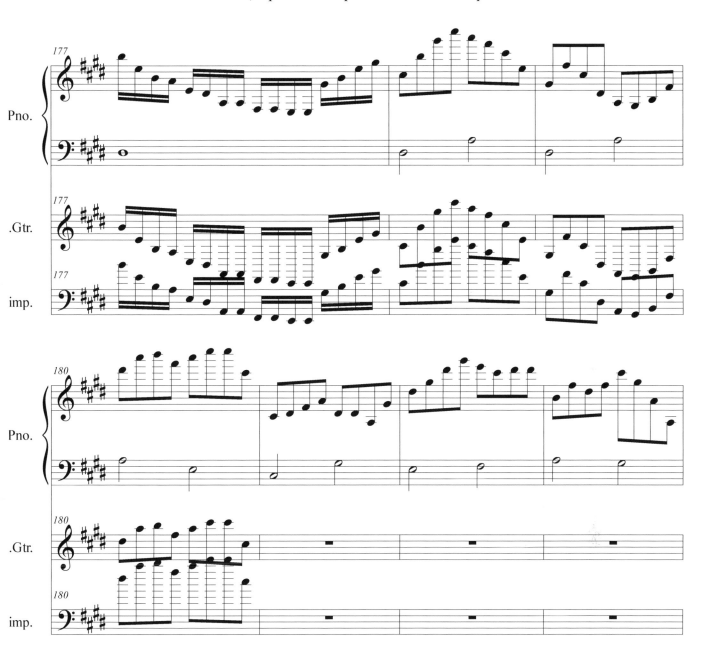

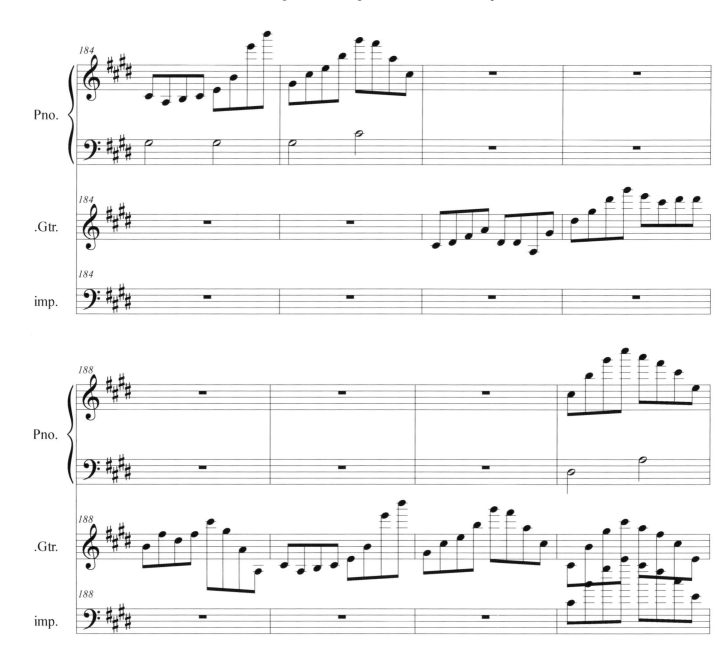

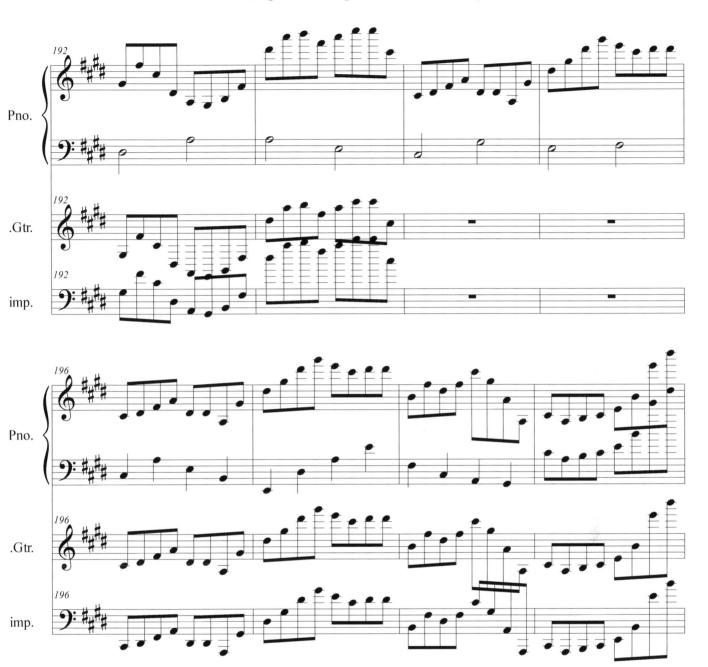

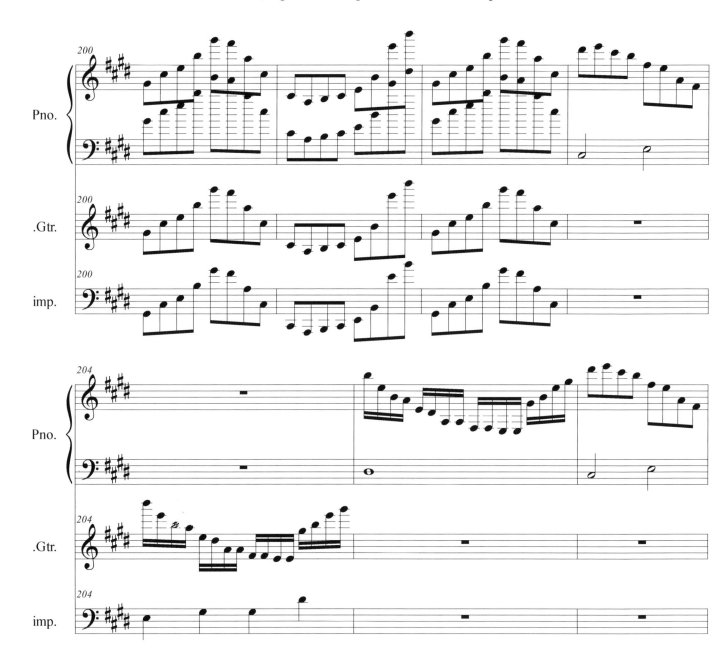

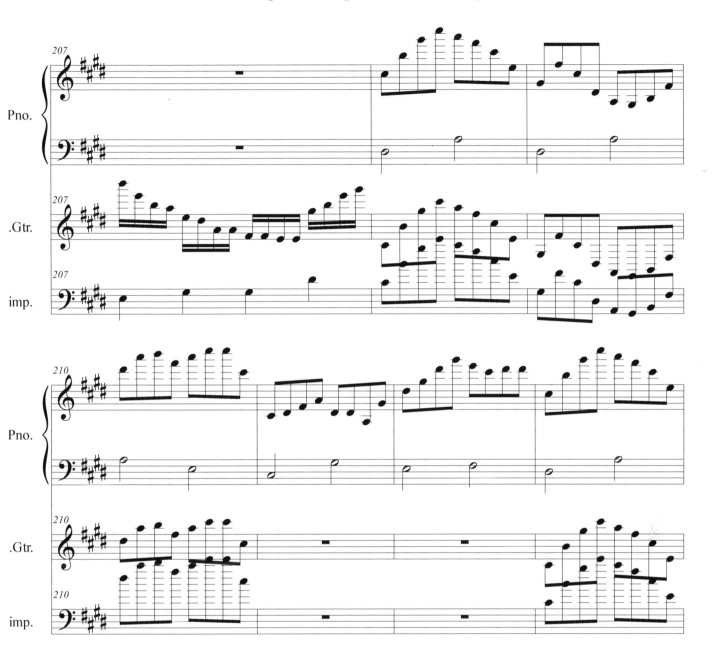

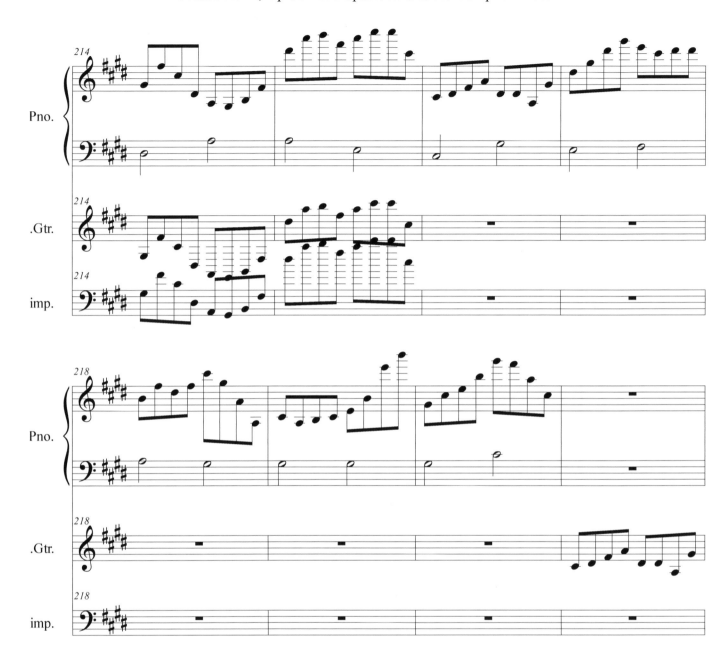

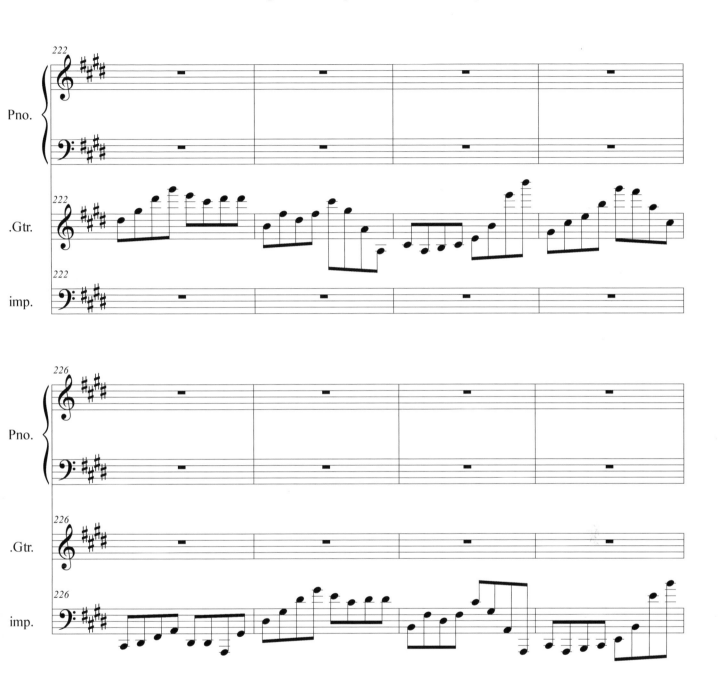

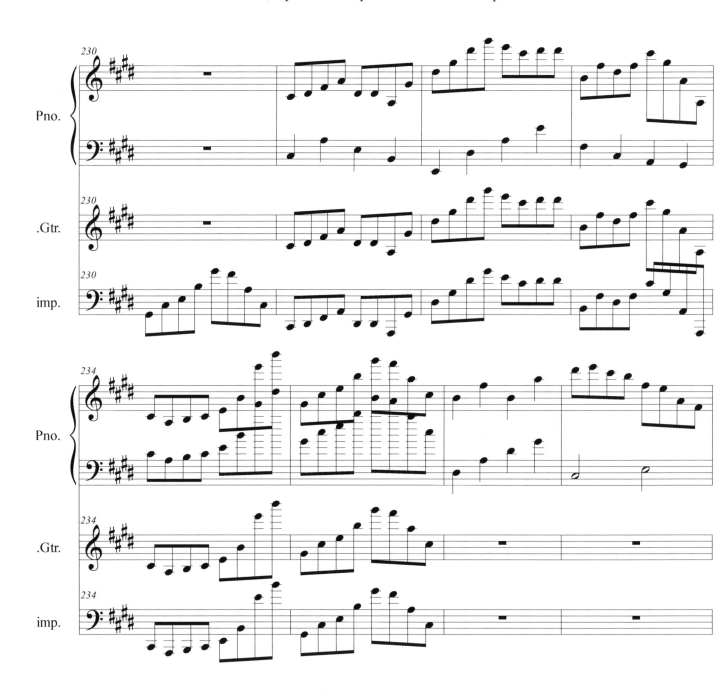

Sonata No 21, Op 81 - The Sparrows and the Camphor Trees

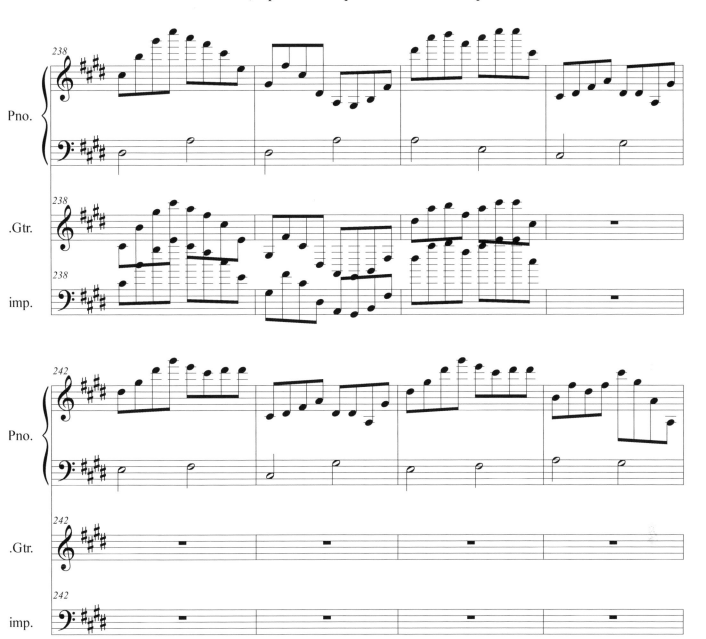

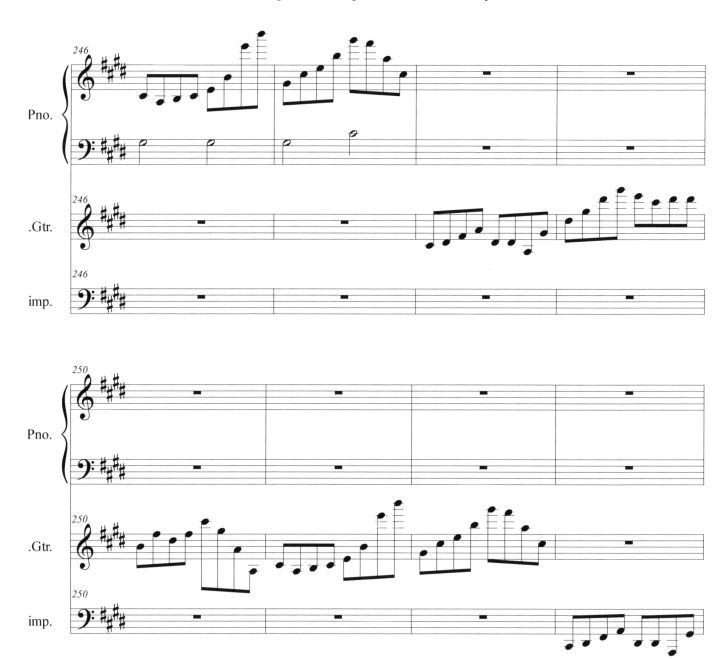

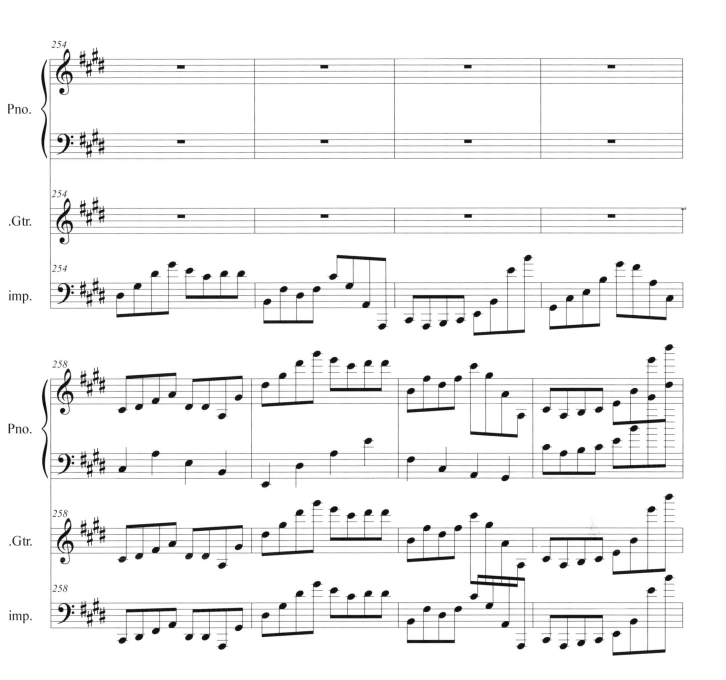

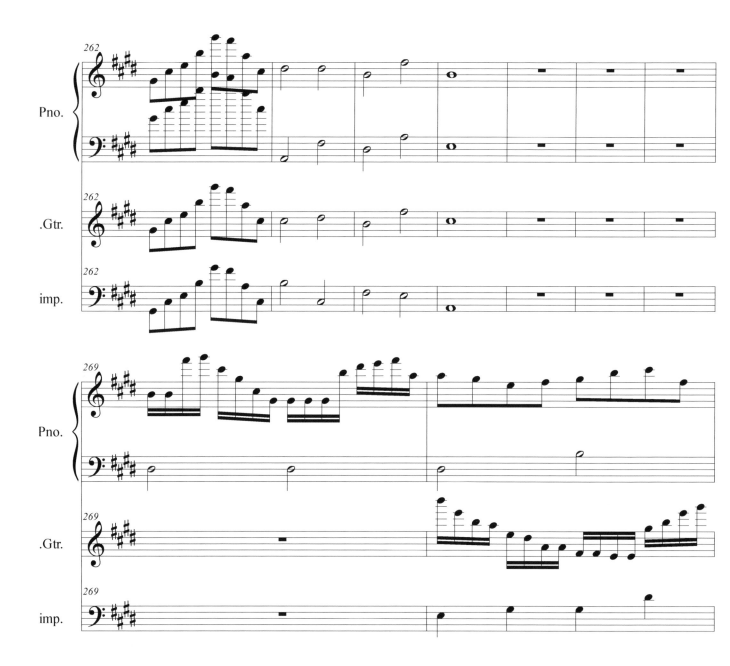

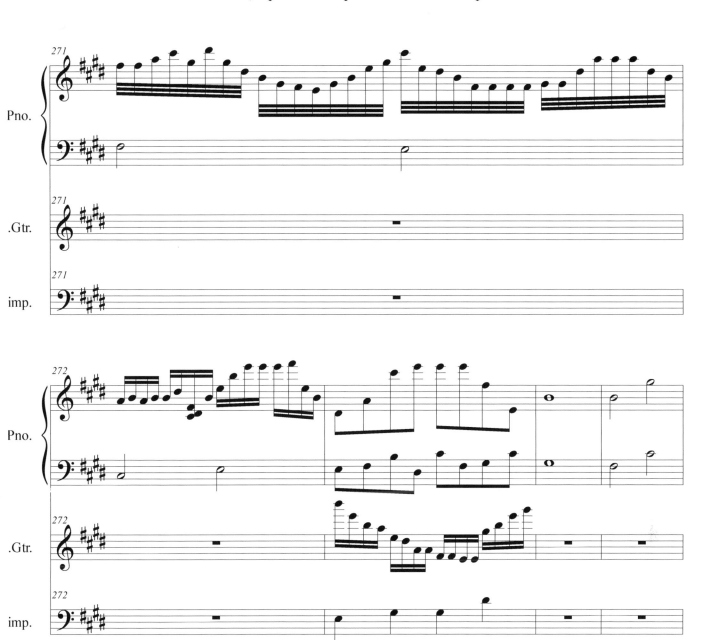

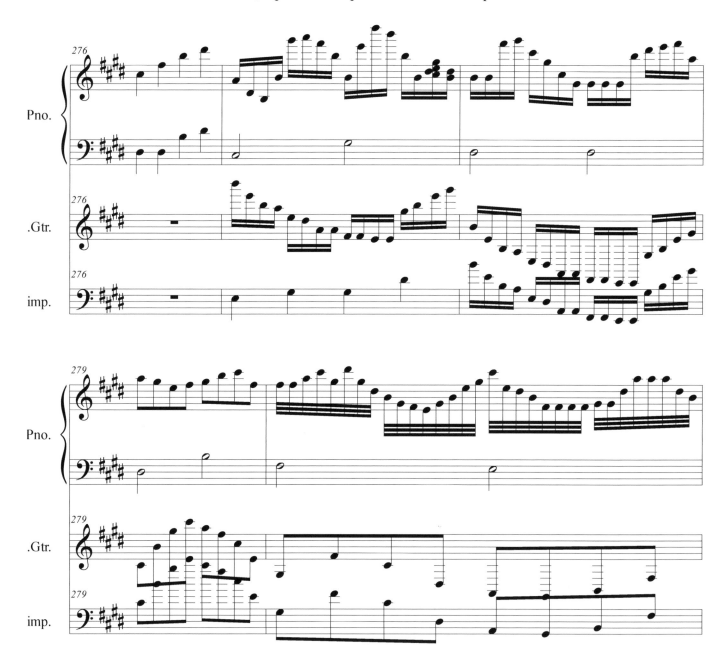

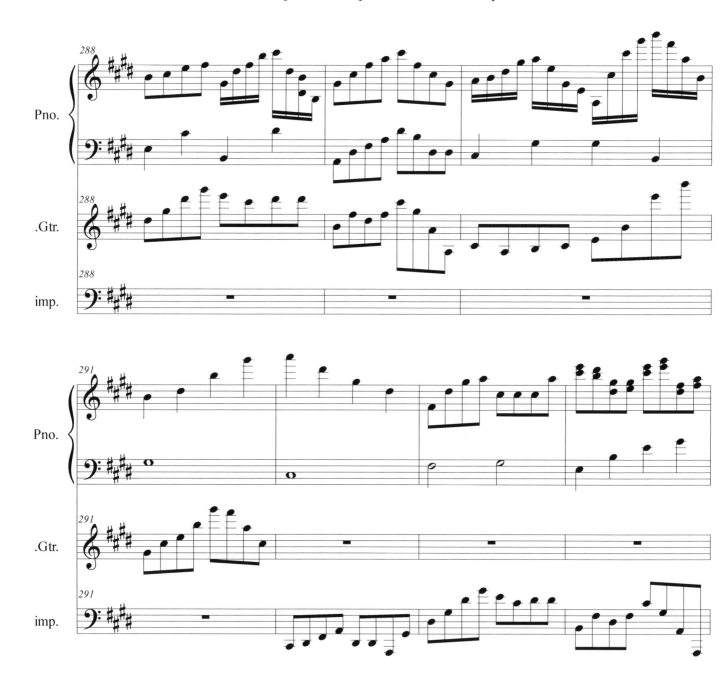

Sonata No 21, Op 81 - The Sparrows and the Camphor Trees

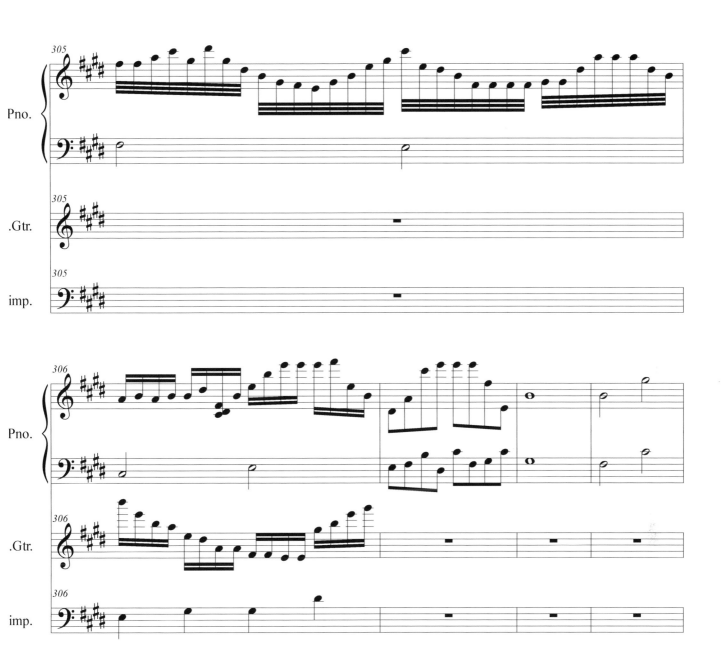

Sonata No 21, Op 81 - The Sparrows and the Camphor Trees

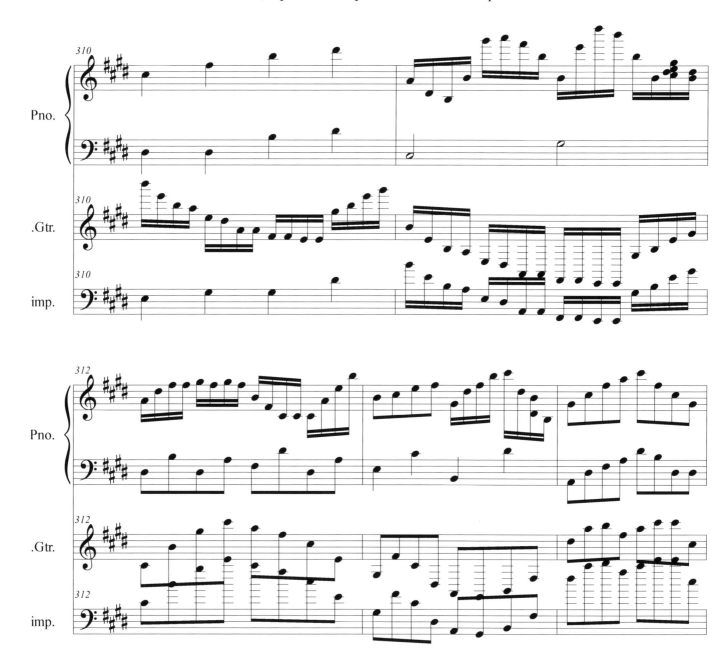

Sonata No 21, Op 81 - The Sparrows and the Camphor Trees

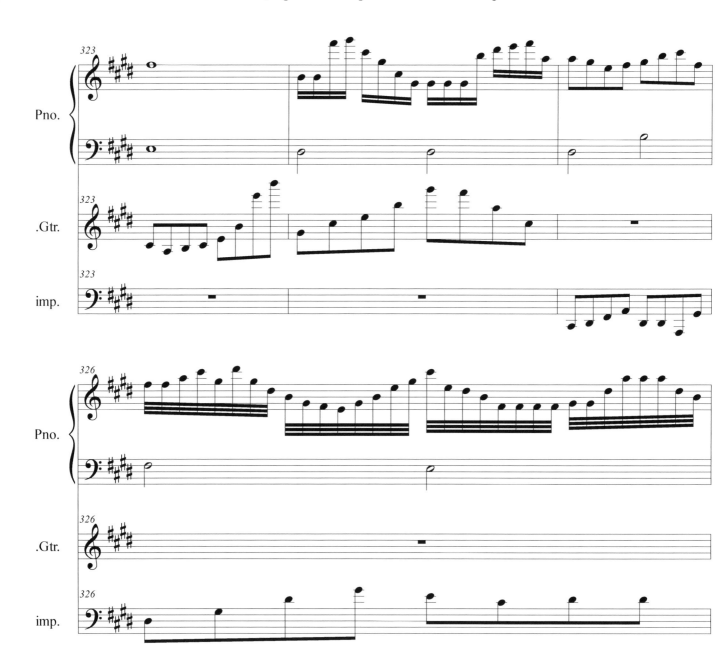

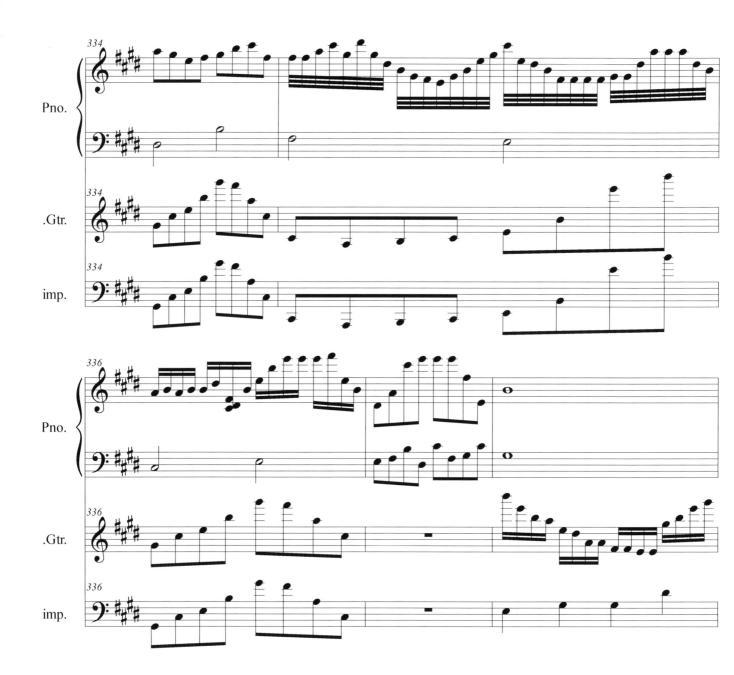

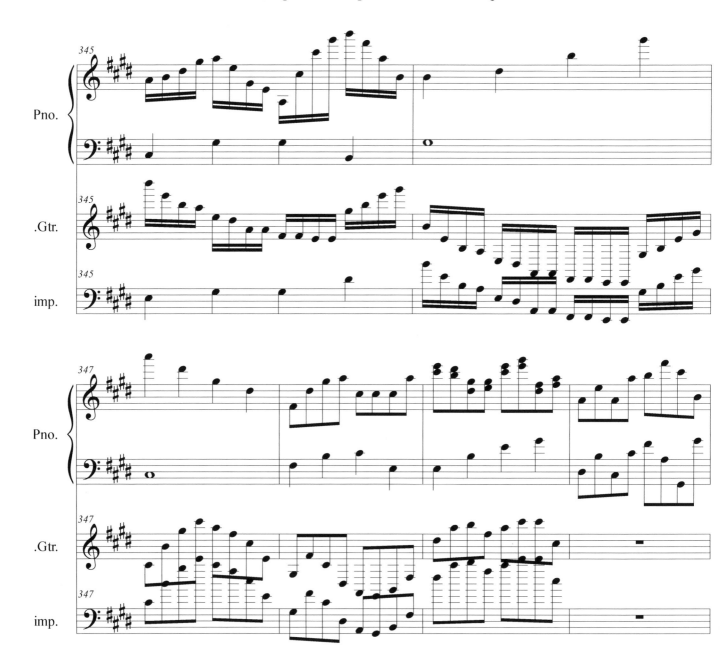

Sonata No 21, Op 81 - The Sparrows and the Camphor Trees

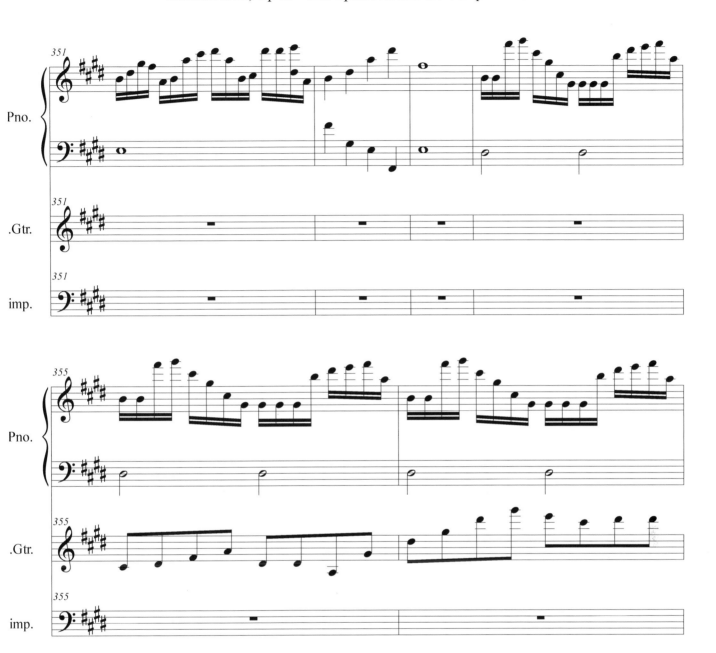

51

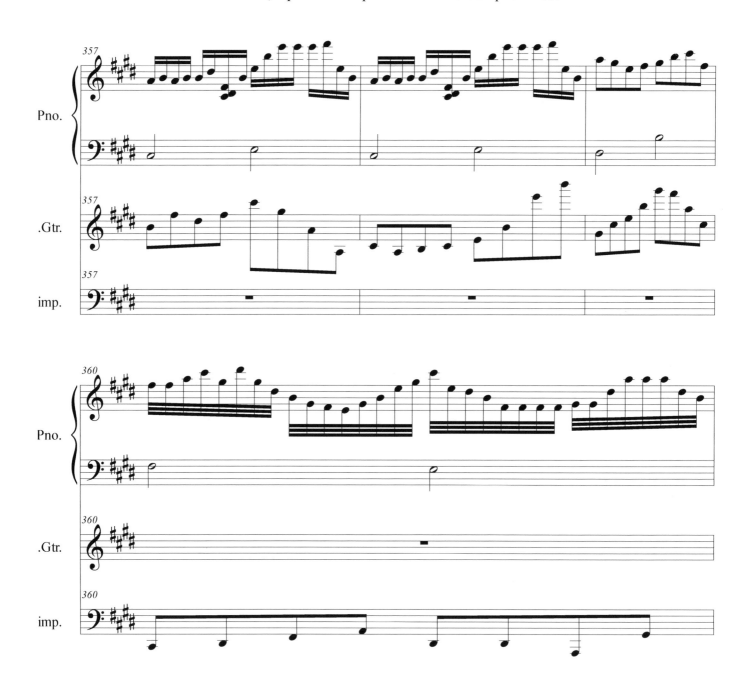

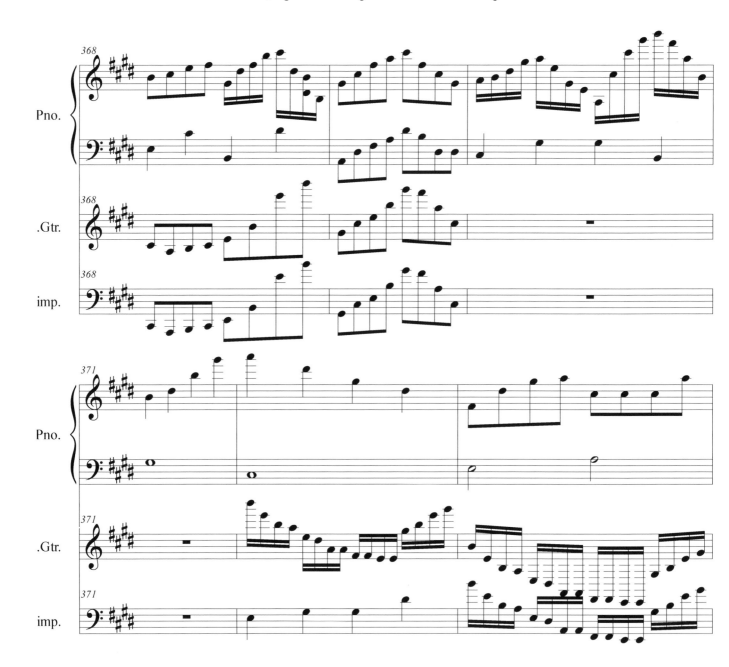

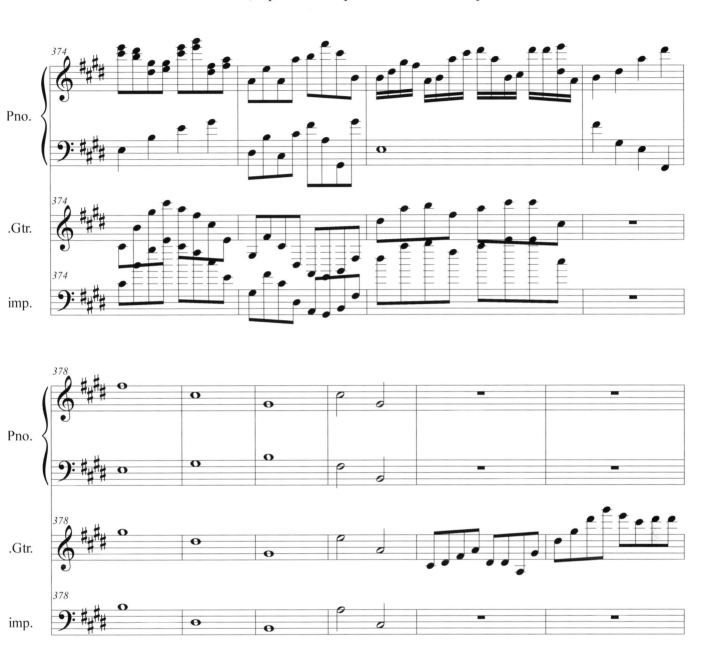

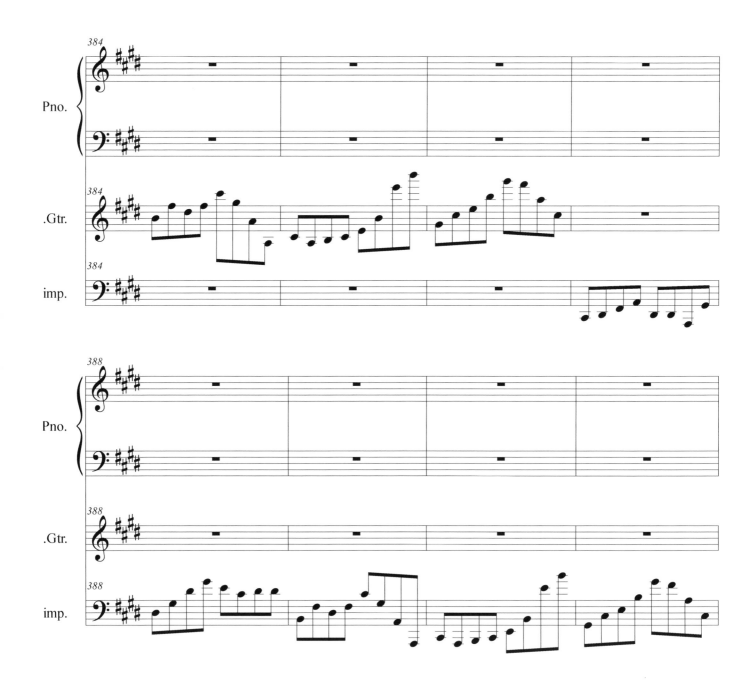

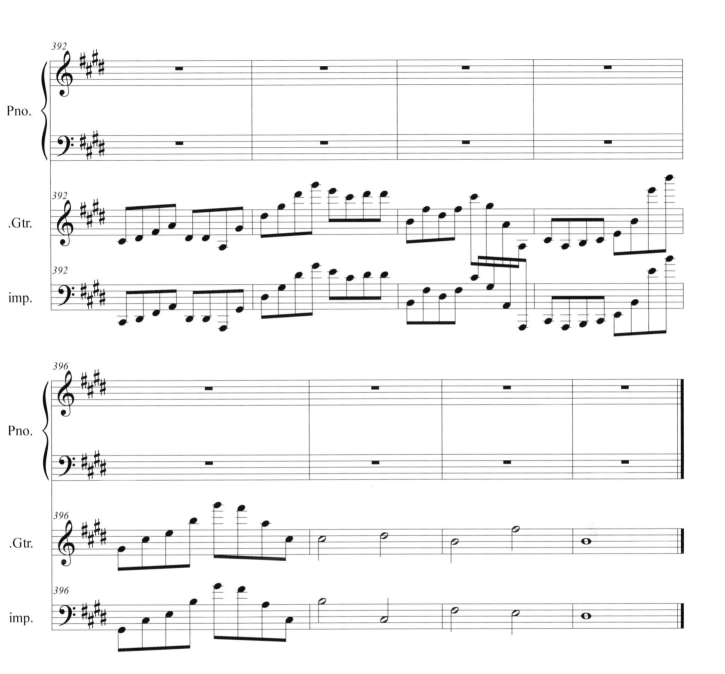

Sonata No 22, Op 263 - For the Sake of Humanity-Part 1

Dr. Anis I. Milad

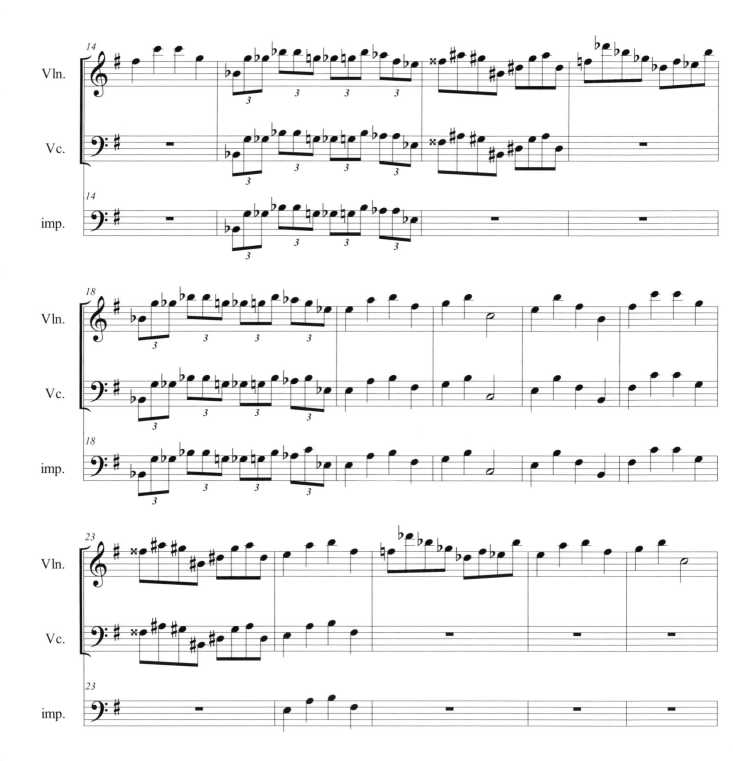

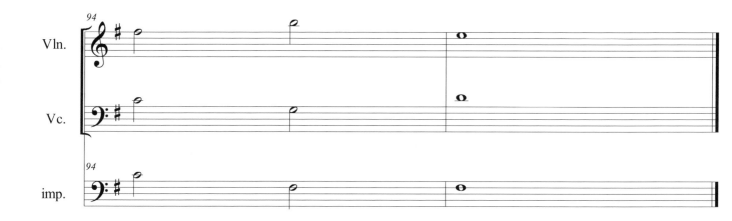

Sonata No 22, Op 263 - For the Sake of Humanity-Part 2

Dr. Anis I. Milad

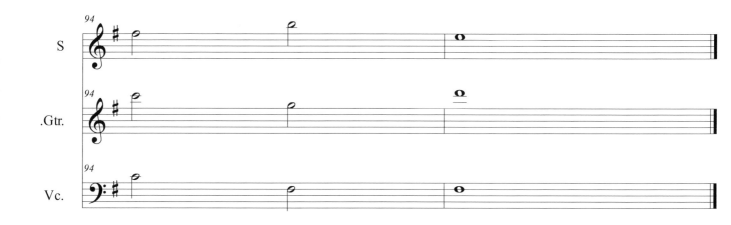

Sonata No 22, Op 263 - For the Sake of Humanity - Part 3

Dr. Anis I. Milad

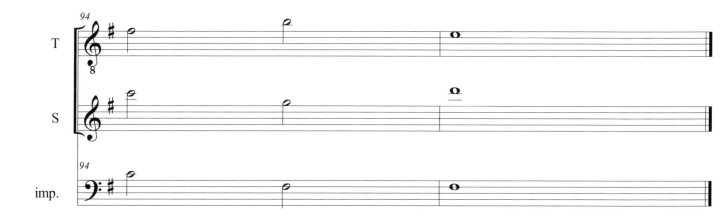

Sonata No 23, Op 264 - I Walk Alone - Part 1

Dr. Anis I. Milad

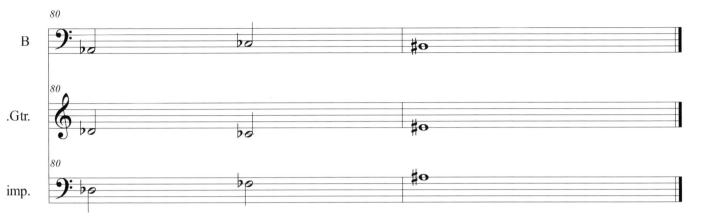

Sonata No 23, Op 264 - I Walk Alone - Part 2

Dr. Anis I. Milad

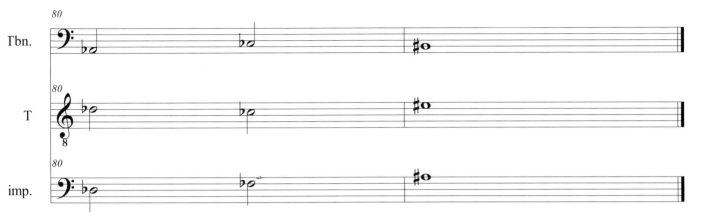

Sonata No 23, Op 264 - I Walk Alone - Part 3

Dr. Anis I. Milad

Sonata No 24, Op 268 - Life - Part 1

Dr. Anis I. Milad

Sonata No 24, Op 268 - Life - Part 1

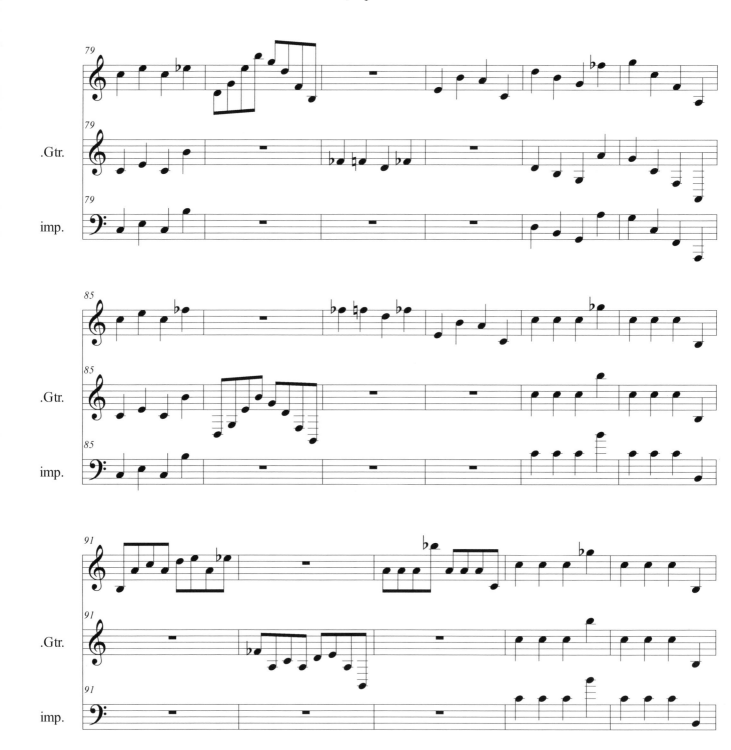

Sonata No 24 - Part 2

Dr. Anis I. Milad

Sonata No 24 - Part 2

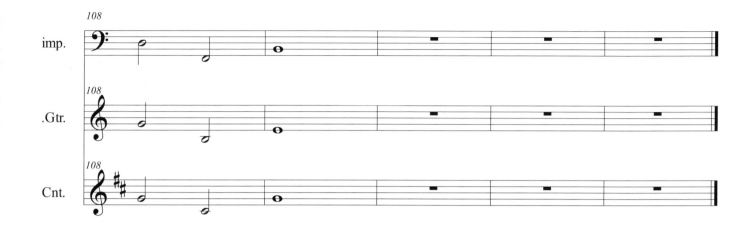

Sonata No 24 - Part 3

Dr. Anis I. Milad

Sonata No 24 - Part 3

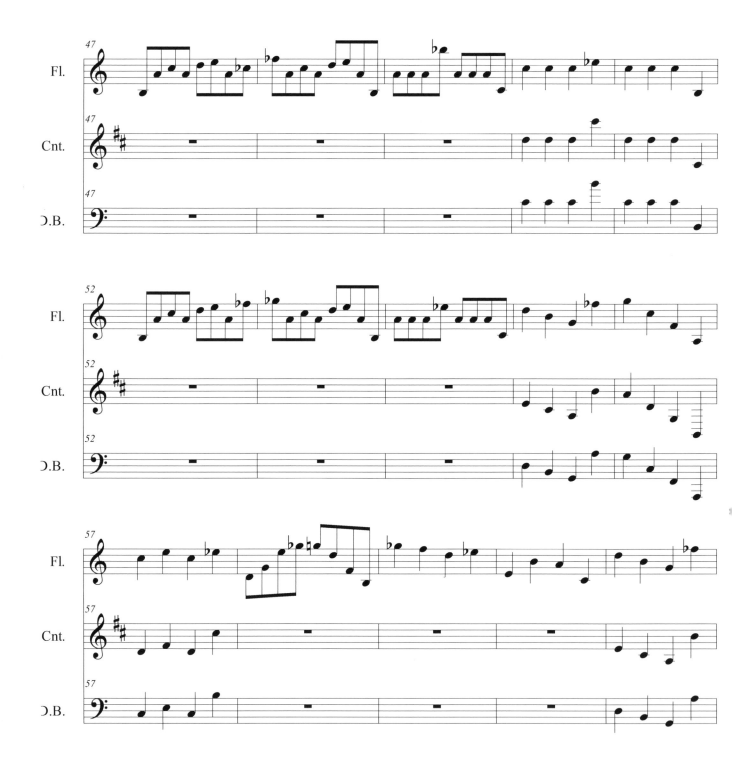

Sonata No 25 - Indispensable Moments - Part 1

Dr. Anis I. Milad

Score

Sonata No 25 - Indispensable Moments - Part 2

Dr. Anis I. Milad

Sonata No 25 - Indispensable Moments - Part 3

Dr. Anis I. Milad

Sonata No 26, Op 273 - Prayer to the Holy Spirit-Part 1

Dr. Anis I.
Milad

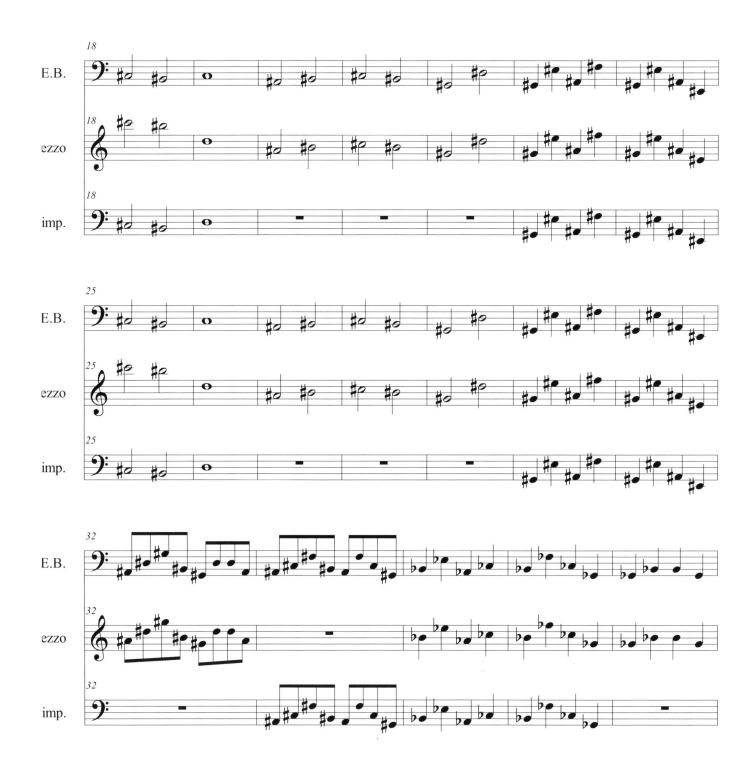

Sonata No 26, Op 273 - Prayer to the Holy Spirit-Part 2

Dr. Anis I. Milad

Sonata No 26, Op 273 - Prayer to the Holy Spirit - Part 3

Dr. Anis I. Milad

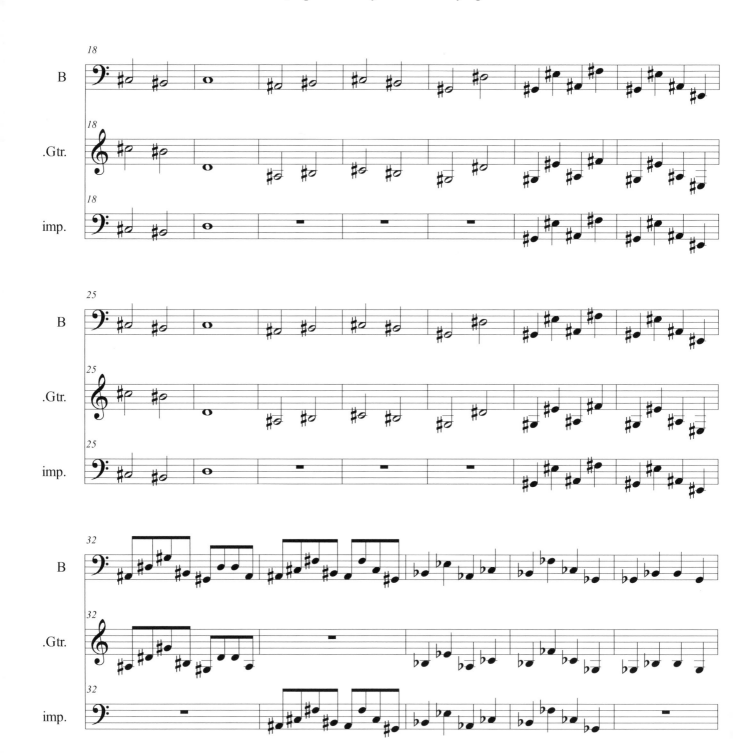

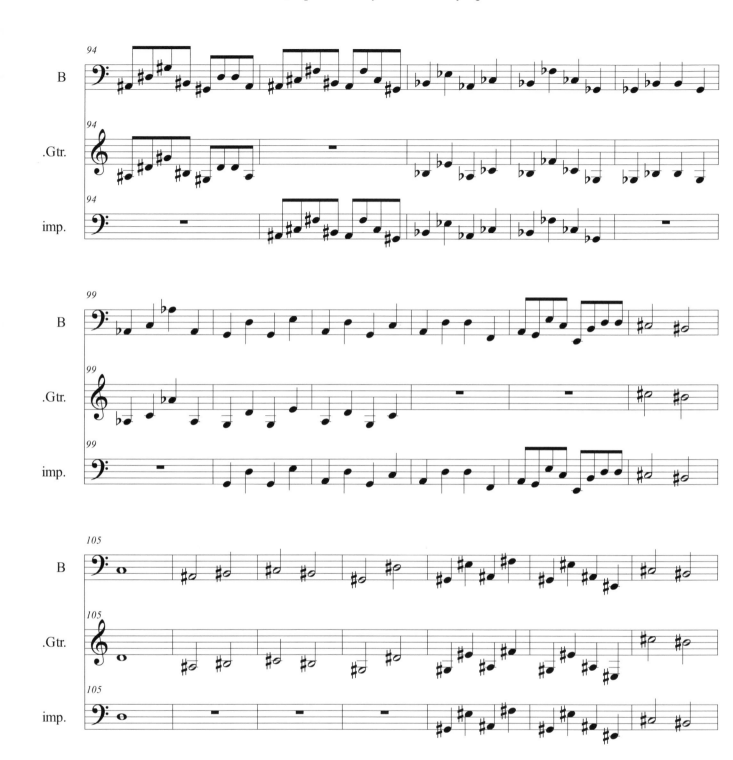

Score

Sonata 27, Op 274 - The Shadow Box of My Reality - Part 1

Dr. Anis I. Milad

Sonata 27, Op 274 - The Shadow Box of My Reality - Part 2

Dr. Anis I. Milad

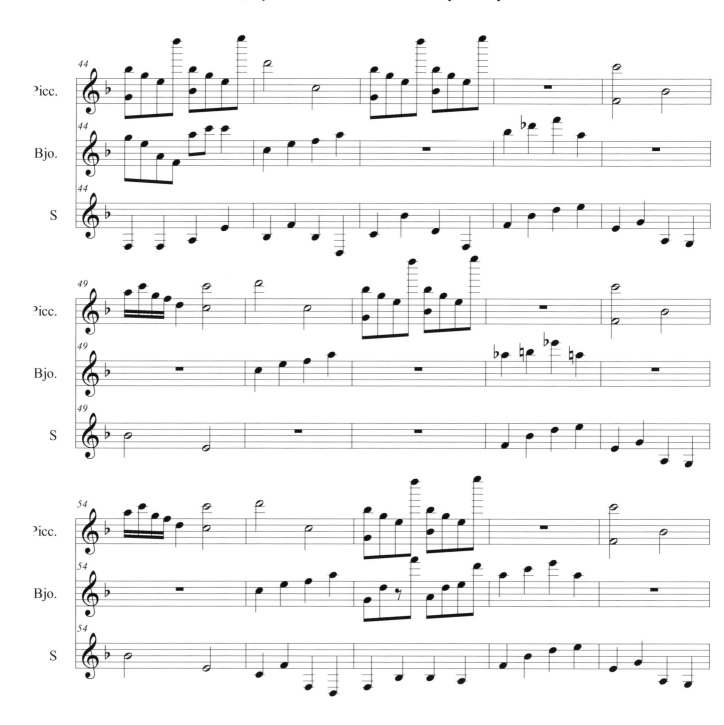

Sonata 27, Op 274 - The Shadow Box of My Reality - Part 3

Dr. Anis I. Milad

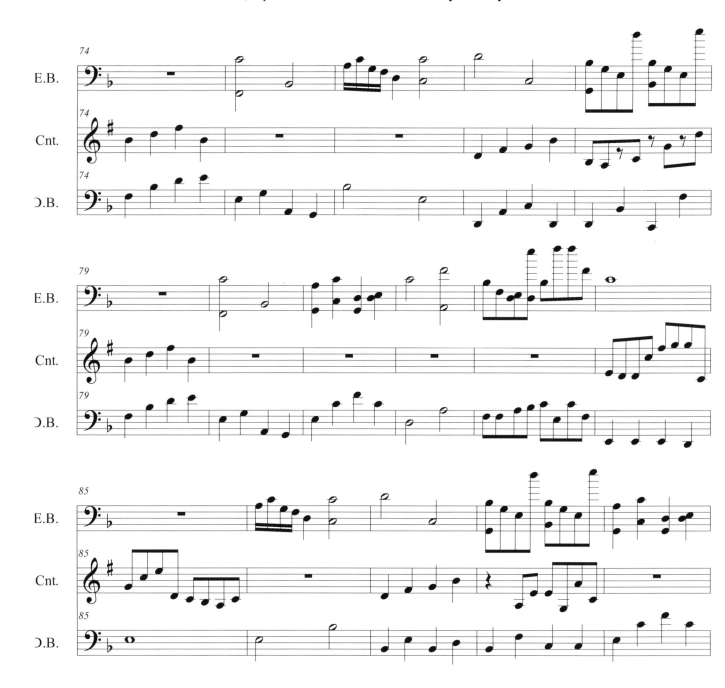

Sonata No 28, Op 275 - Echoes of Abu Simbel Temple - Part 1

Dr. Anis I. Milad

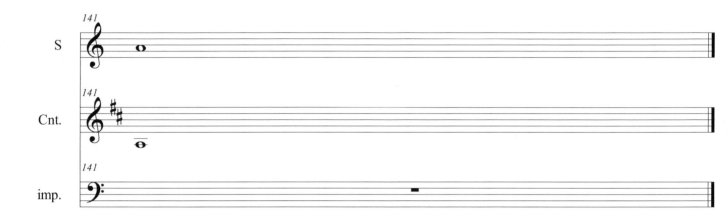

Sonata No 28, Op 275 - Echoes of Abu Simbel Temple - Part 2

Dr. Anis I. Milad

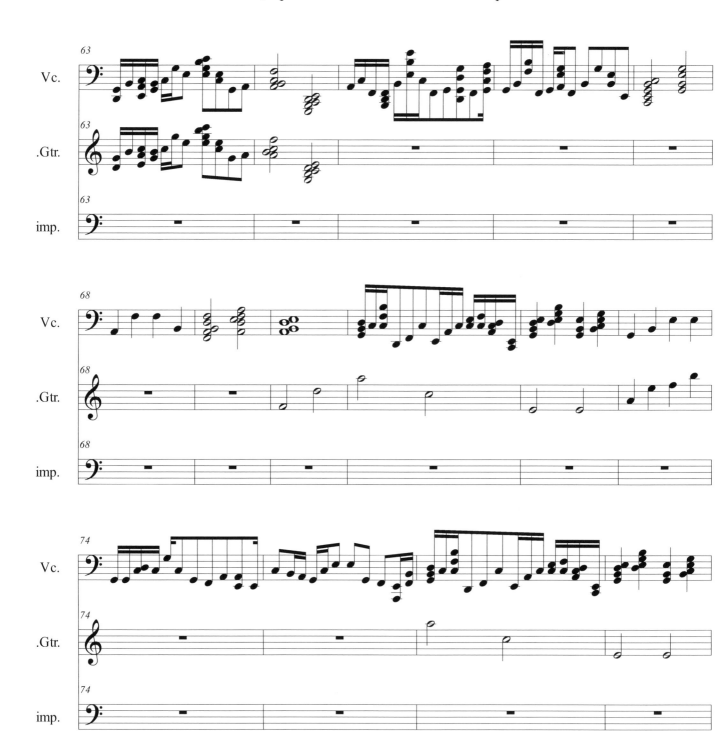

Sonata No 28, Op 275 - Echoes of Abu Simbel Temple - Part 3

Dr. Anis I. Milad

Sonata No 29, Op 276 - Brief Emotion - Part 1

Dr. Anis I. Milad

Sonata No 29, Op 276 - Brief Emotion - Part 1

Sonata No 29, Op 276 - Brief Emotion - Part 1

Score

Sonata No 29, Op 276 - Brief Emotion - Part 2

Dr. Anis I. Milad

Score

Sonata No 29, Op 276 - Brief Emotion - Part 3

Dr. Anis I. Milad

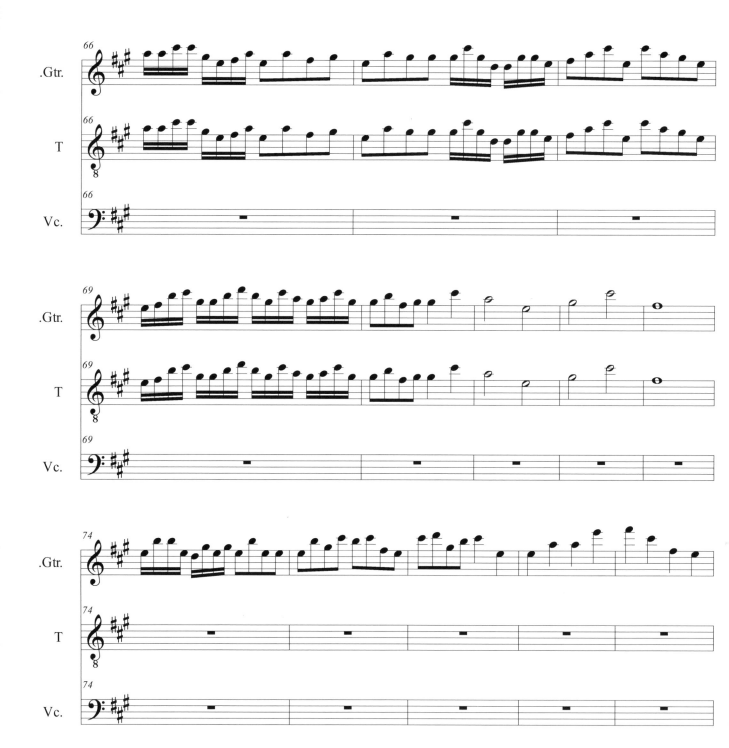

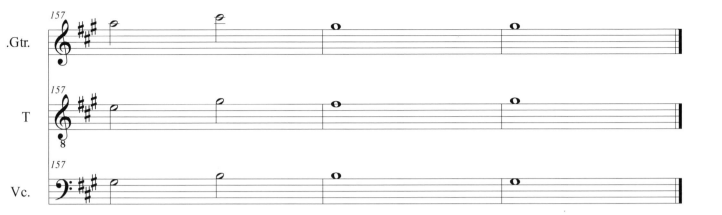

Sonata No 30 - My Woman My Universe - Part 1

Dr. Anis I. Milad

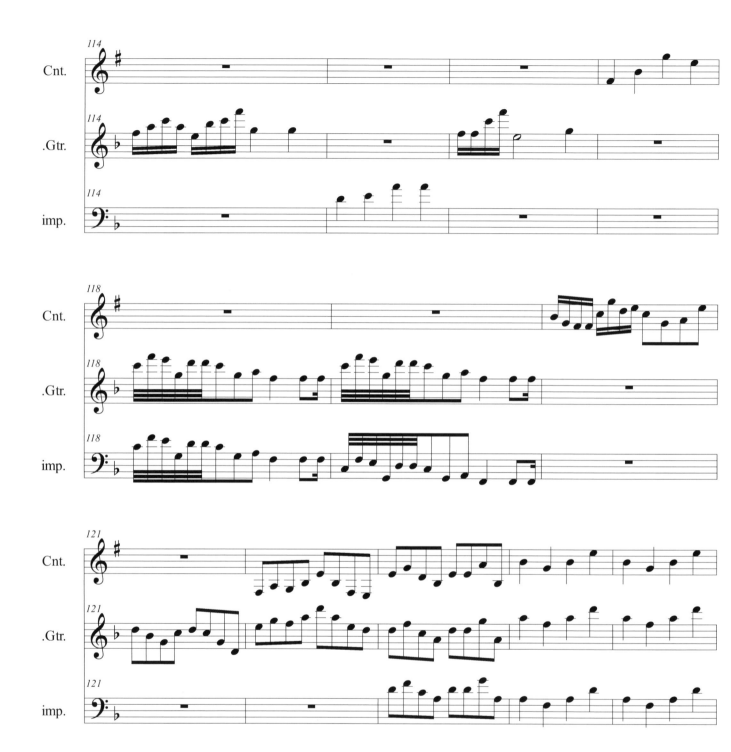

Sonata No 30, My Woman My Universe-Part 2

Dr. Anis I. Milad

Sonata No 30, My Woman My Universe-Part 2

294

Sonata No 30, My Woman My Universe-Part 2

Sonata No 30 - My Woman My Universe - Part 3

Dr. Anis I. Milad

Sonata No 31, Op 278 - The Ingenious Consciousness - Part 1

Dr. Anis I. Milad

Sonata No 31, Op 278 - The Ingenious Consciousness - Part 2

Dr. Anis I. Milad

Sonata No 31, Op 278 - The Ingenious Consciousness - Part 3

Dr. Anis I. Milad

Sonata No 32, Op 279 - Falling On Her Knees - Part 1

Dr. Anis I. Milad

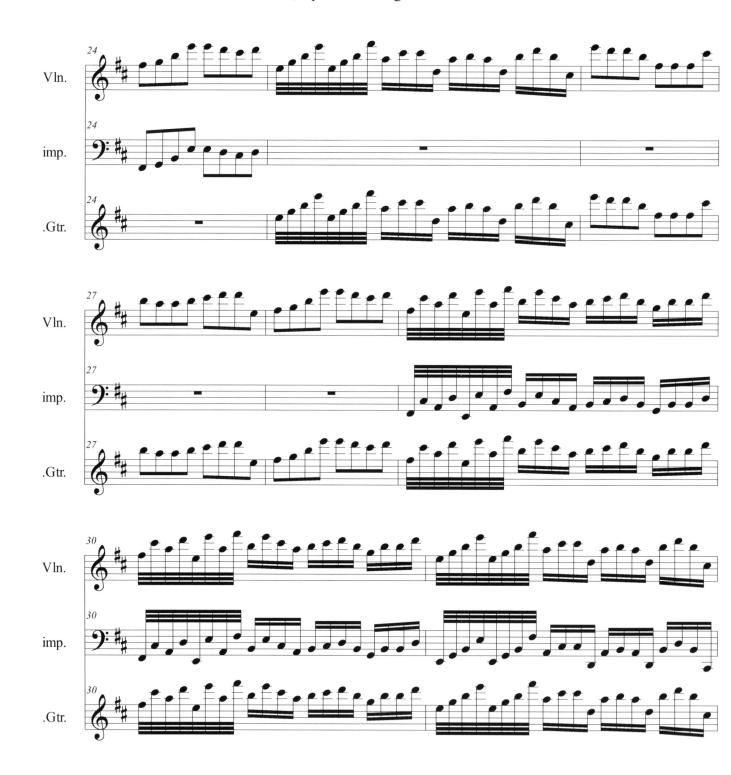

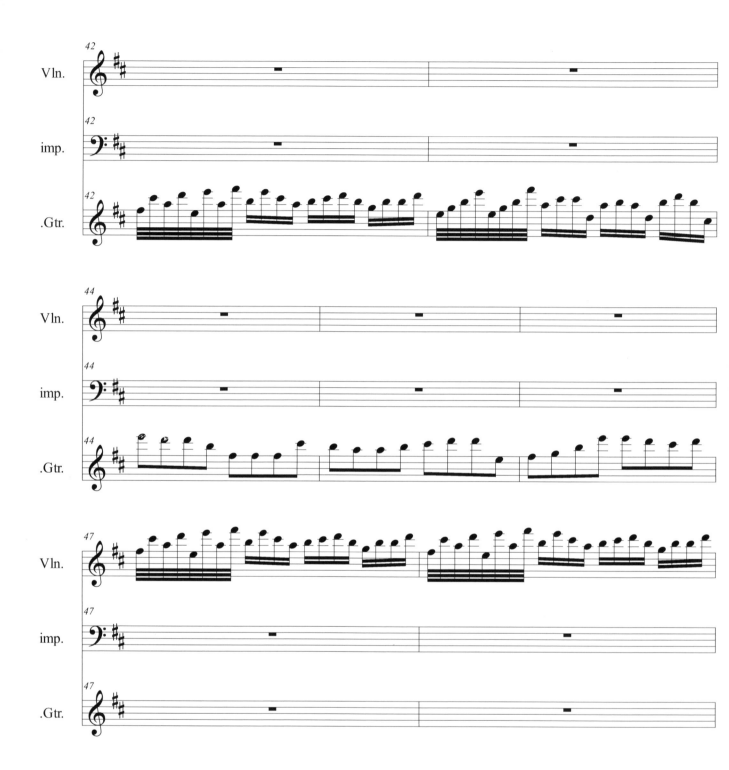

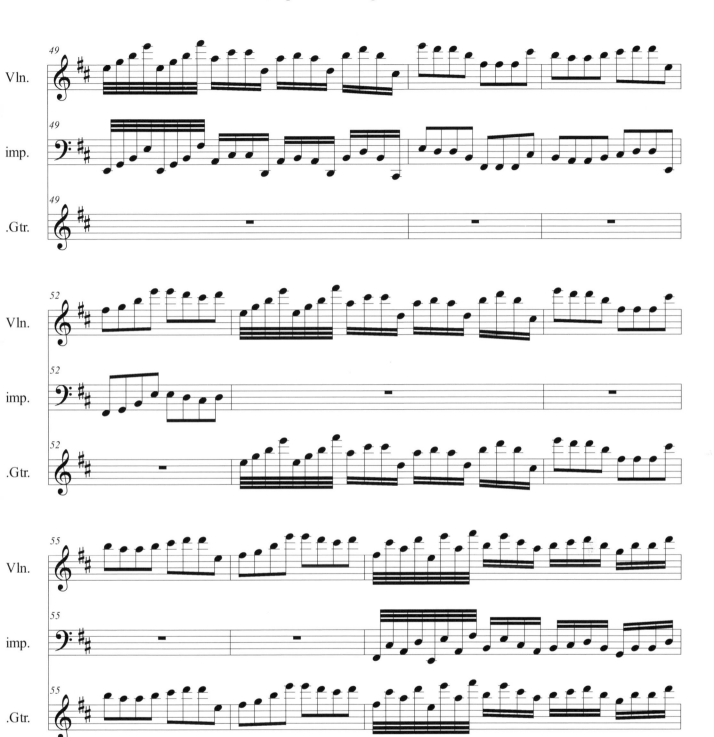

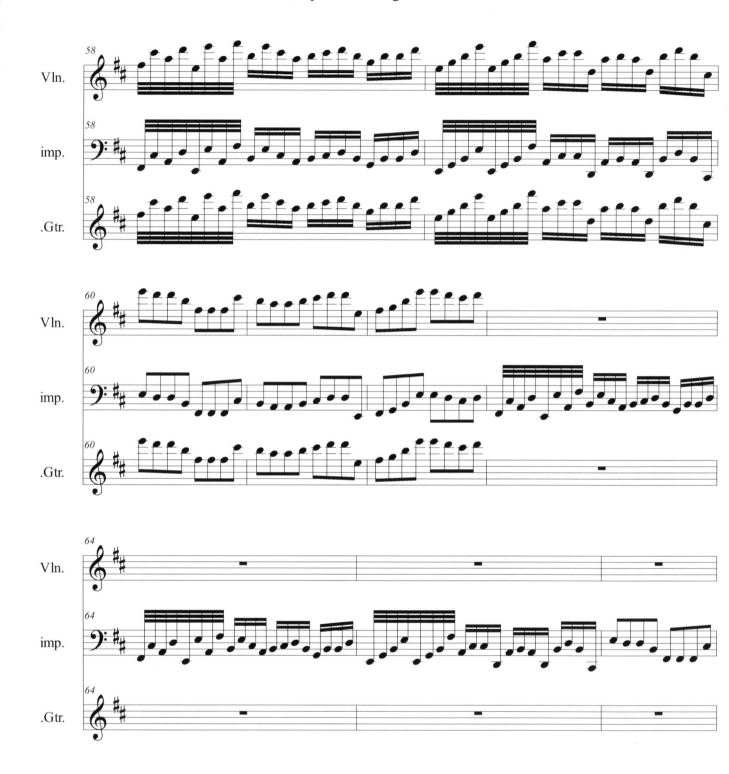

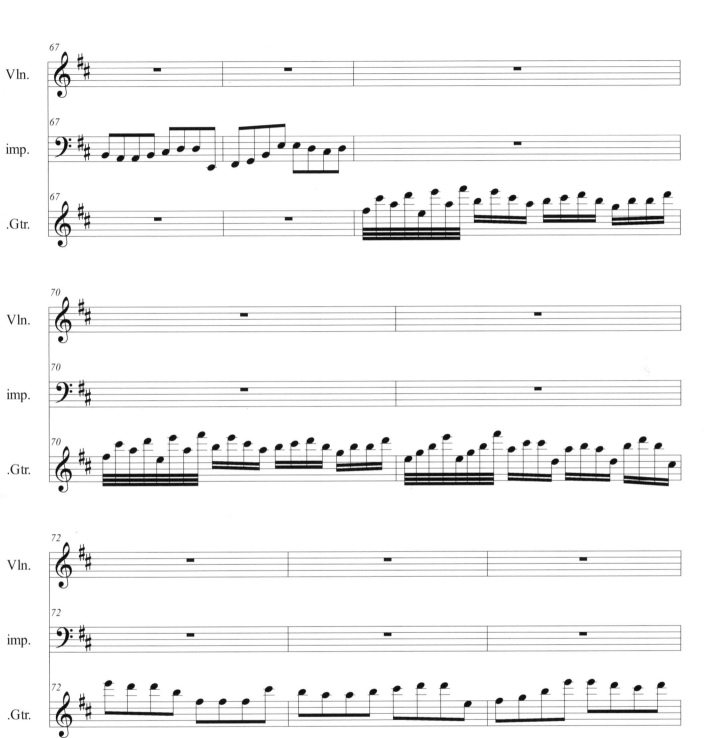

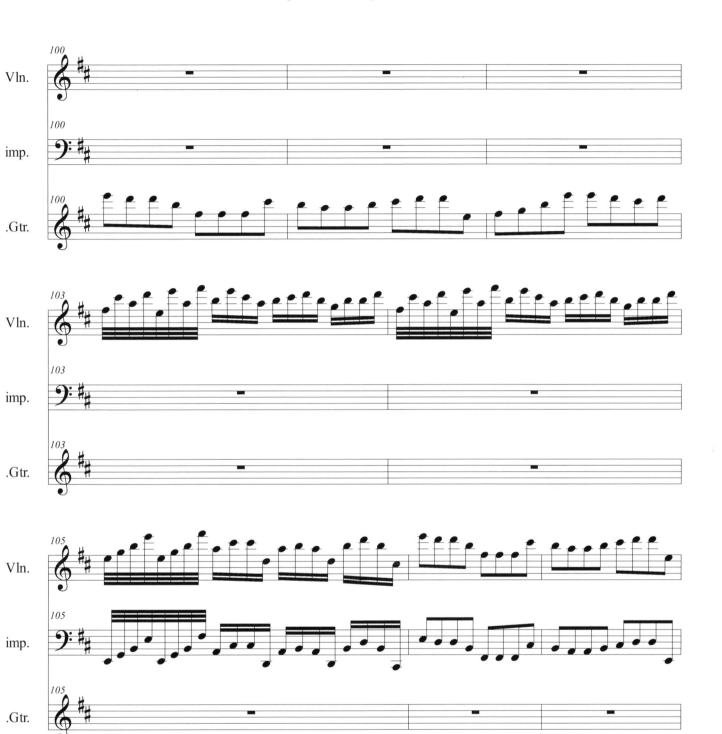

Sonata No 32, Op 279 - Falling On Her Knees - Part 2

Dr. Anis I. Milad

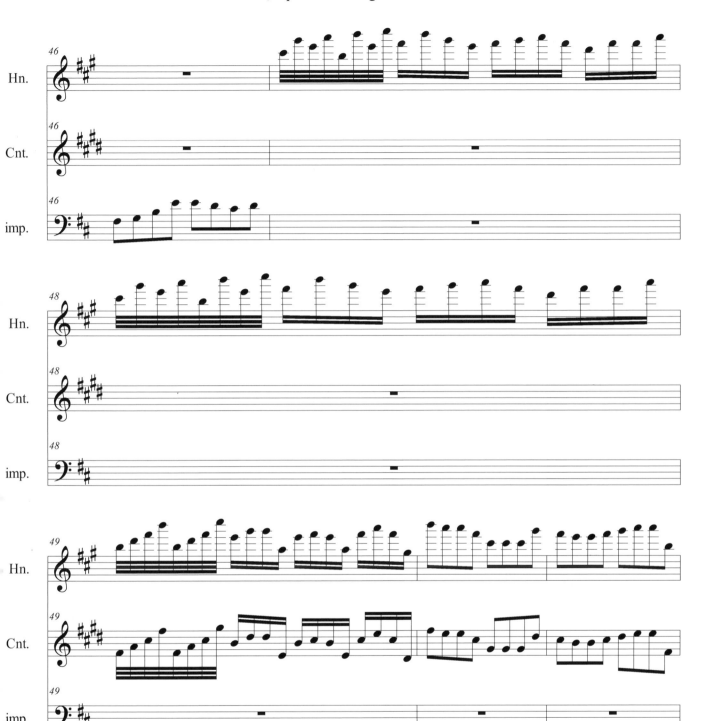

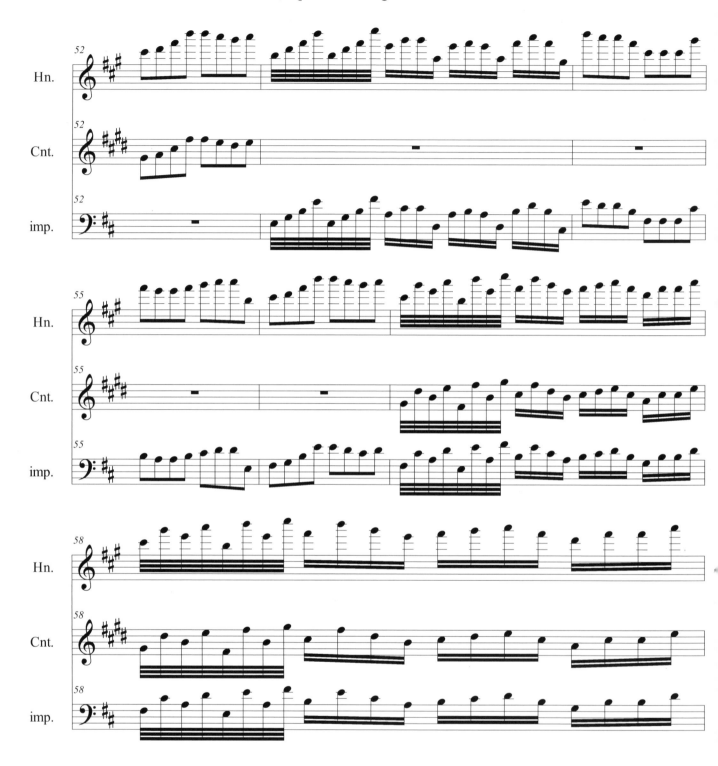

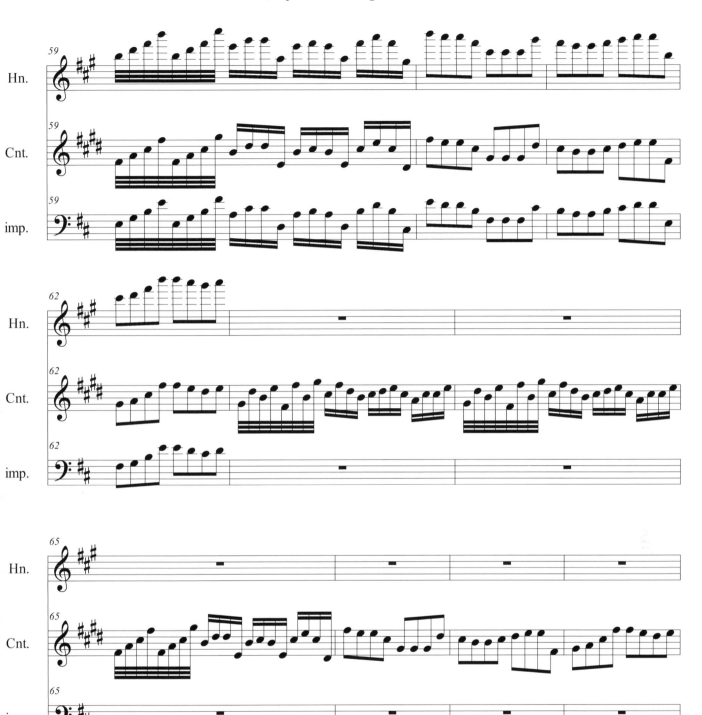

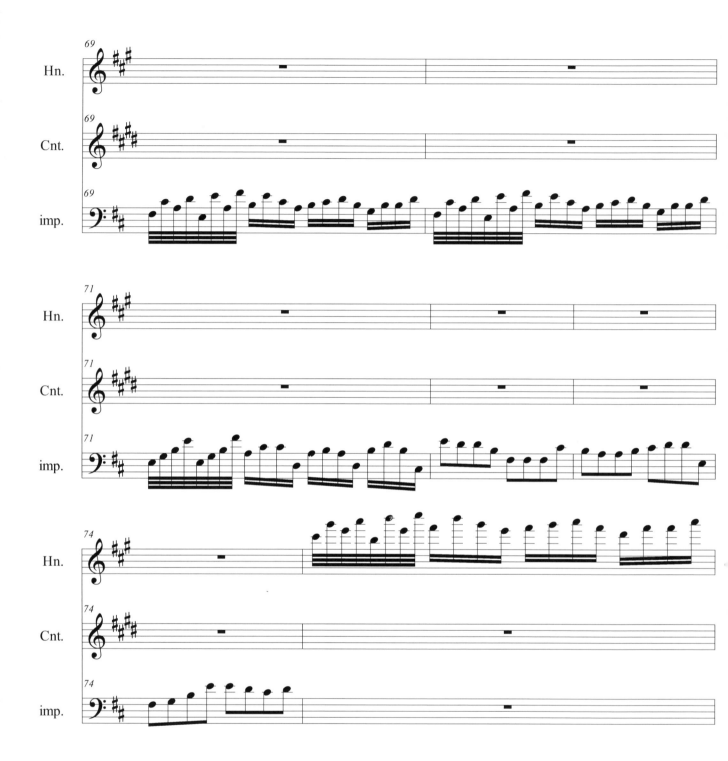

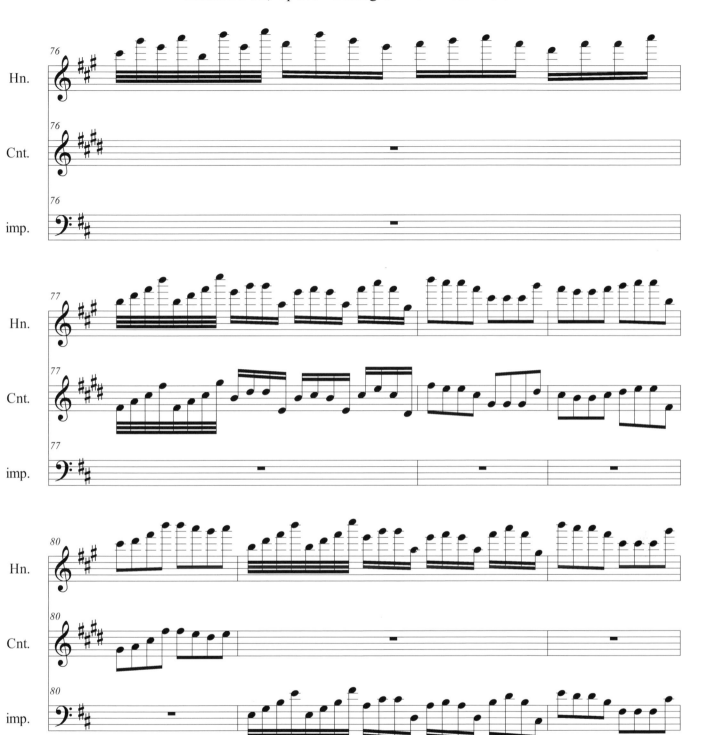

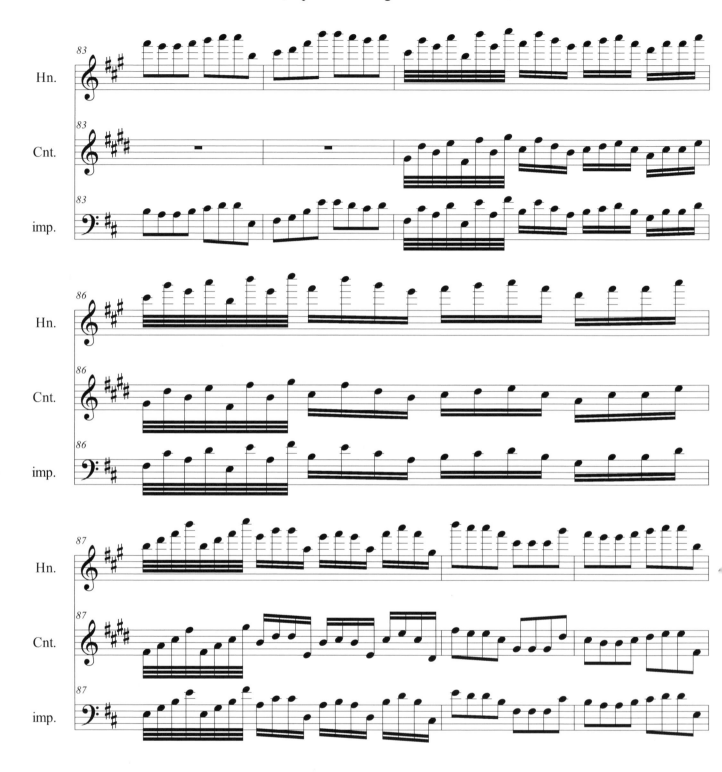

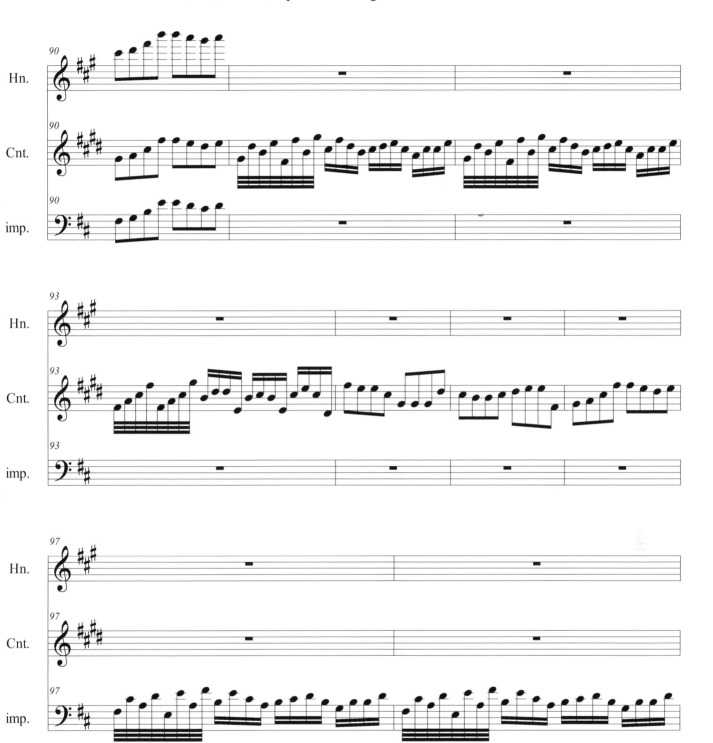

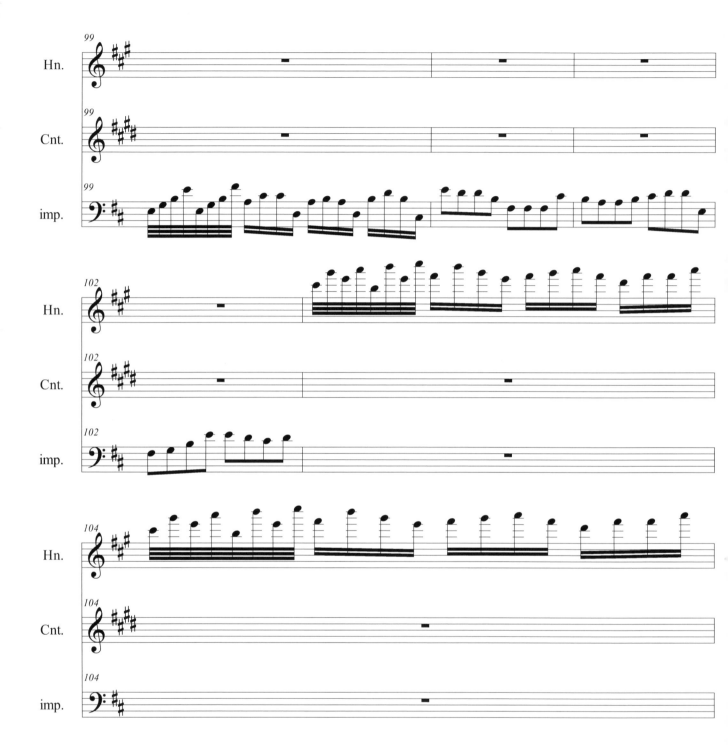

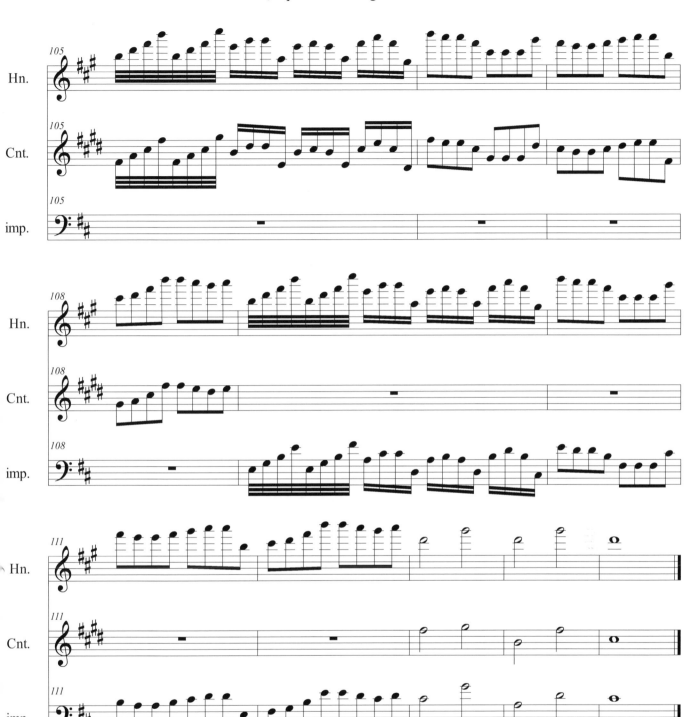

Score

Sonata No 32, Op 279 - Falling On Her Knees - Part 3

Dr. Anis I. Milad

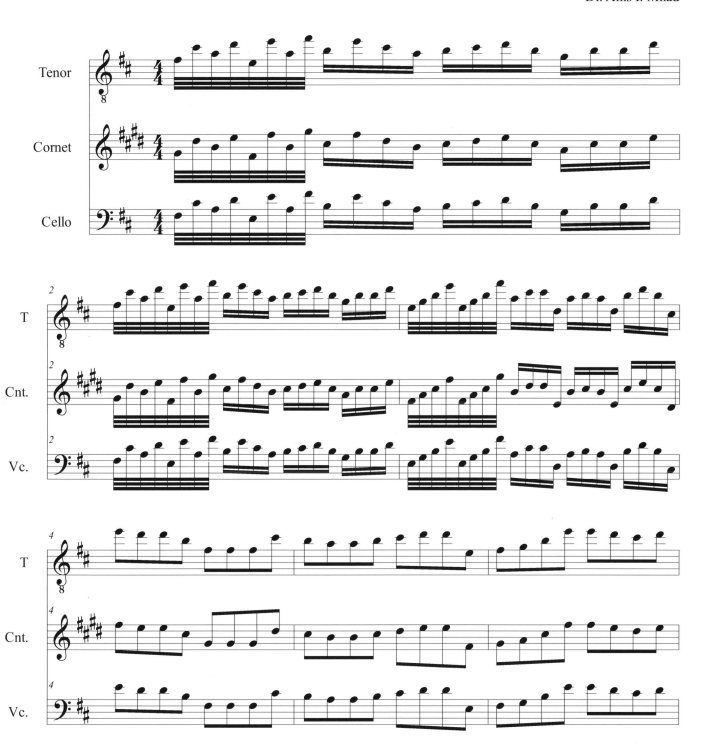

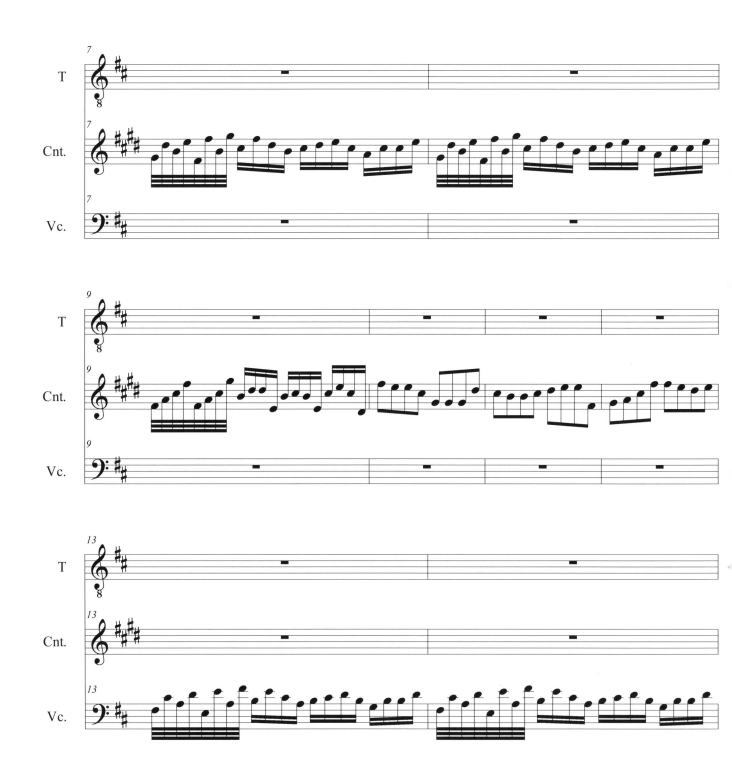

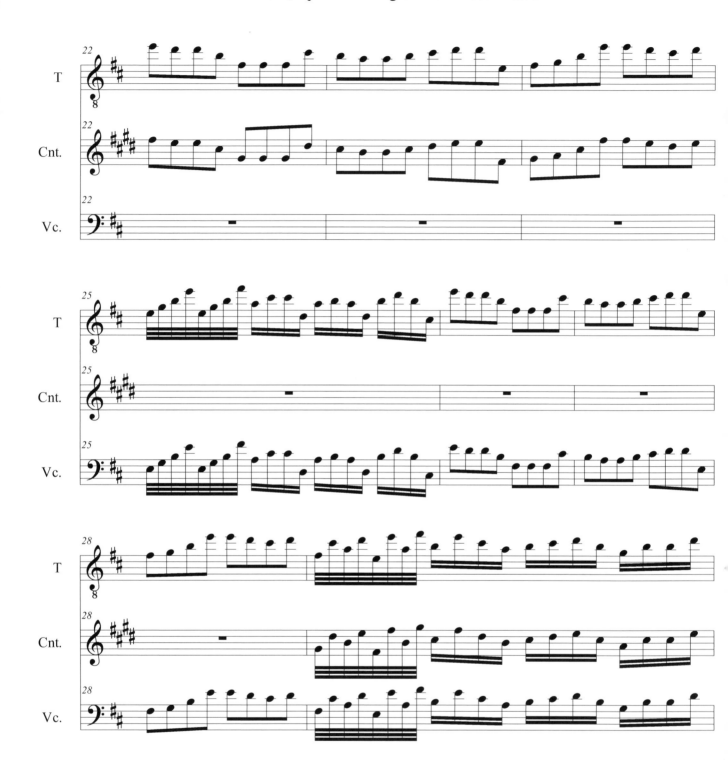

Sonata No 32, Op 279 - Falling On Her Knees - Part 3

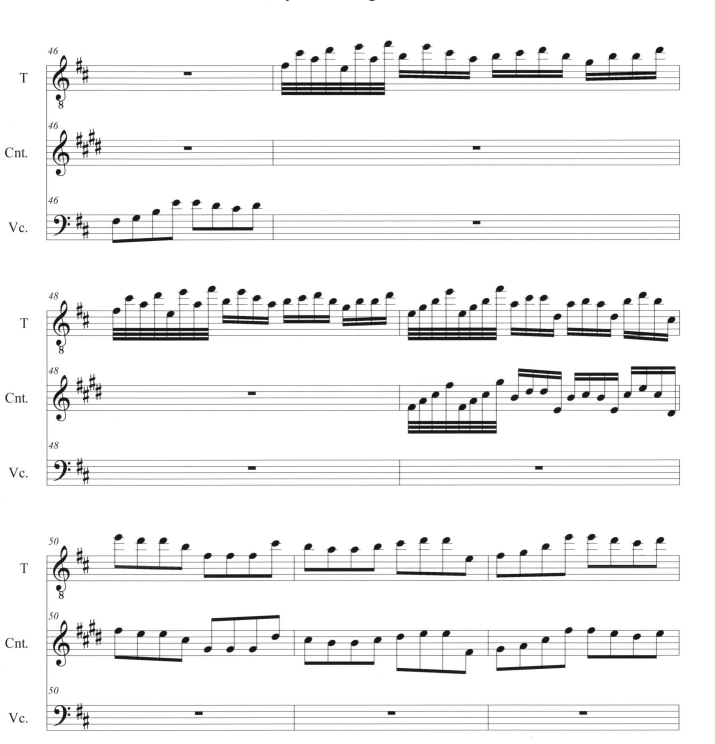

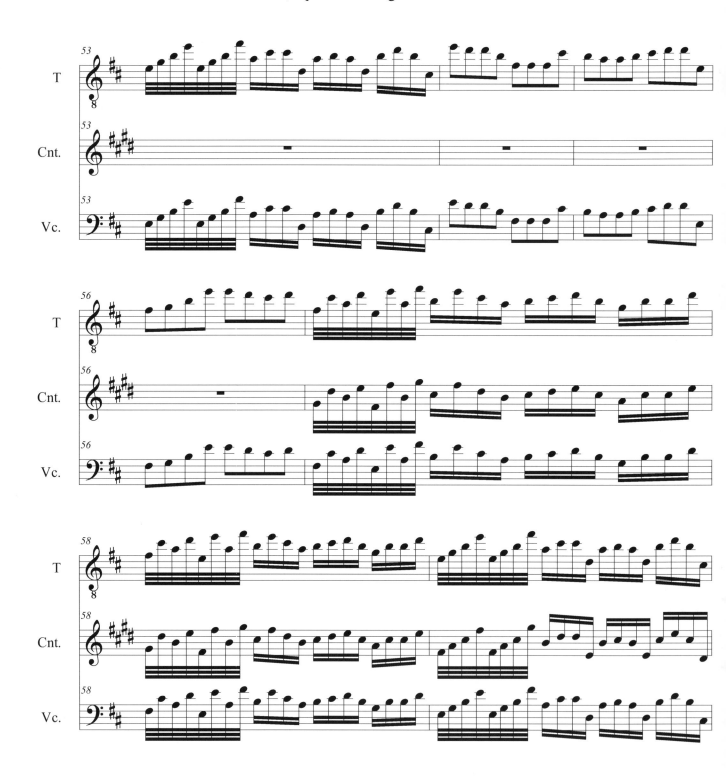

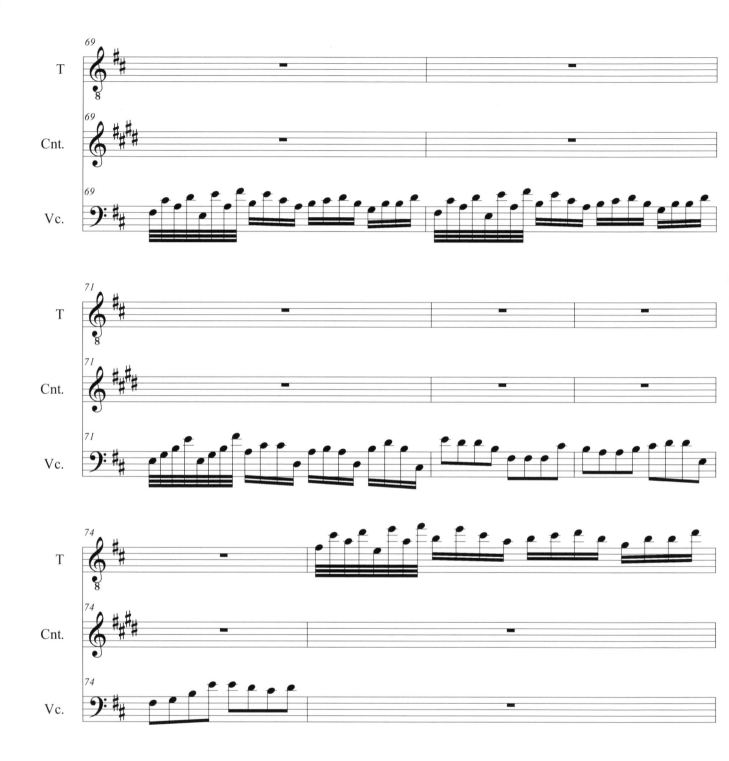

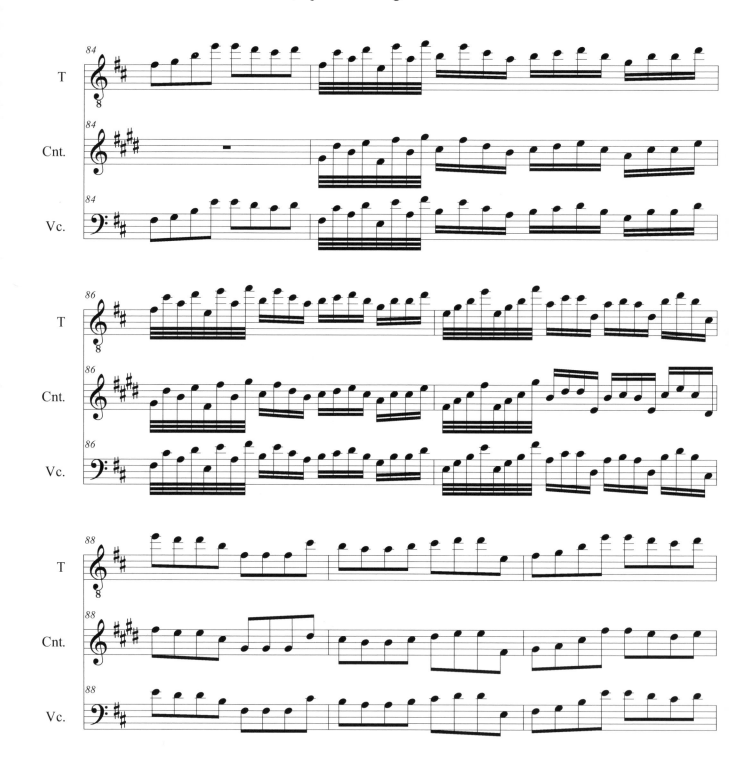

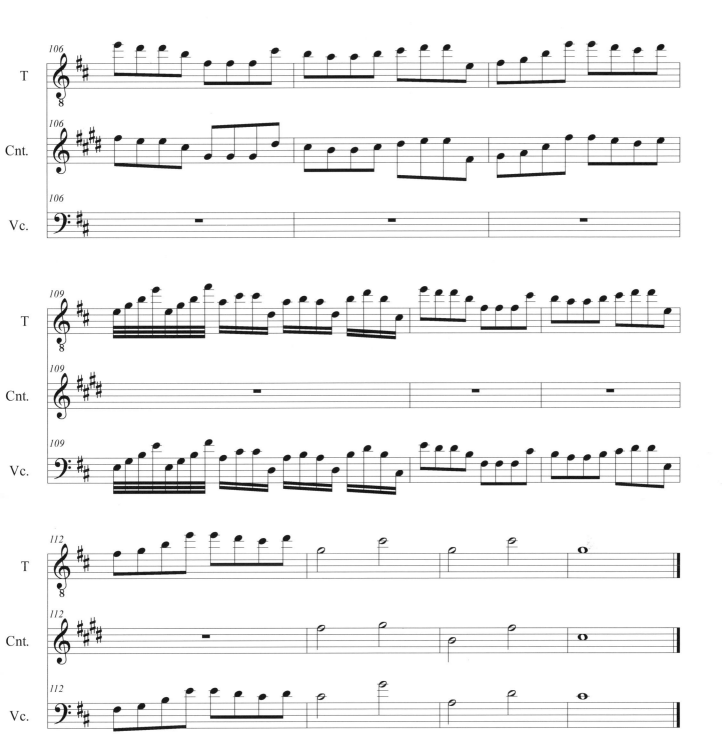

Sonata No 33, Op 280 - The Story of Us - Part 1

Dr. Anis I. Milad

Score

Sonata No 33, Op 280 - The Story of Us - Part 2

Dr. Anis I. Milad

Sonata No 33, Op 280 - The Story of Us - Part 2

Sonata No 33, Op 280 - The Story of Us - Part 2

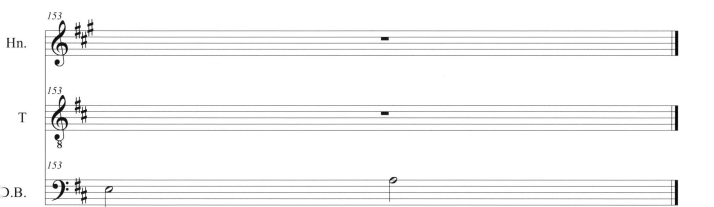

Sonata No 33, Op 280 - The Story of Us - Part 3

Dr. Anis I. Milad

Sonata No 33, Op 280 - The Story of Us - Part 3

417

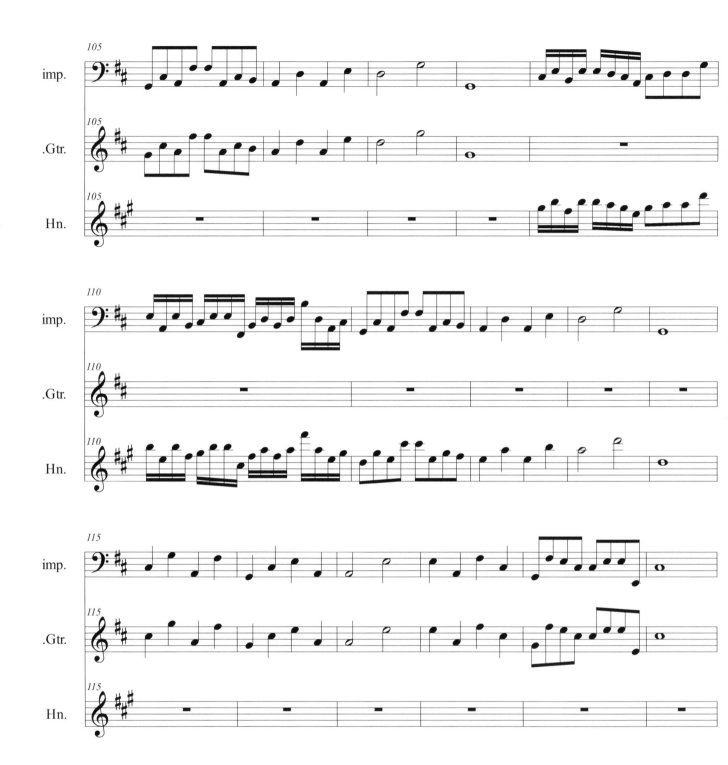

Sonata No 33, Op 280 - The Story of Us - Part 3

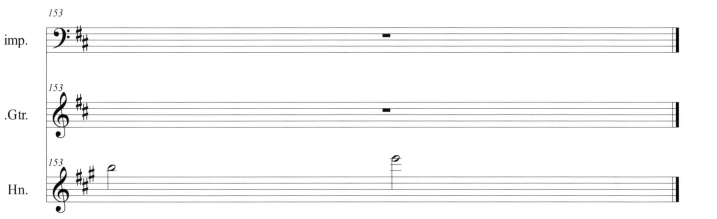

Sonata No 34, Op 281 - Sailing To Eternity - Part 1

Dr. Anis I. Milad

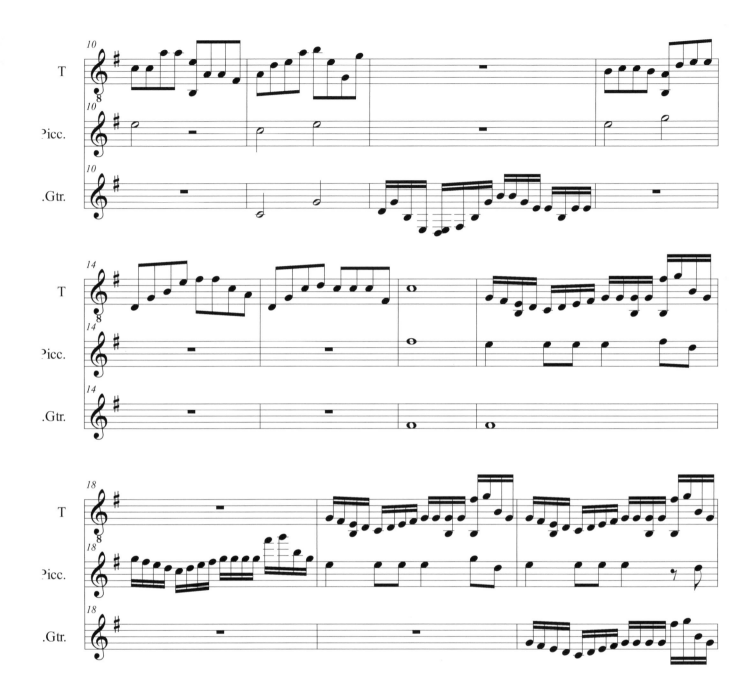

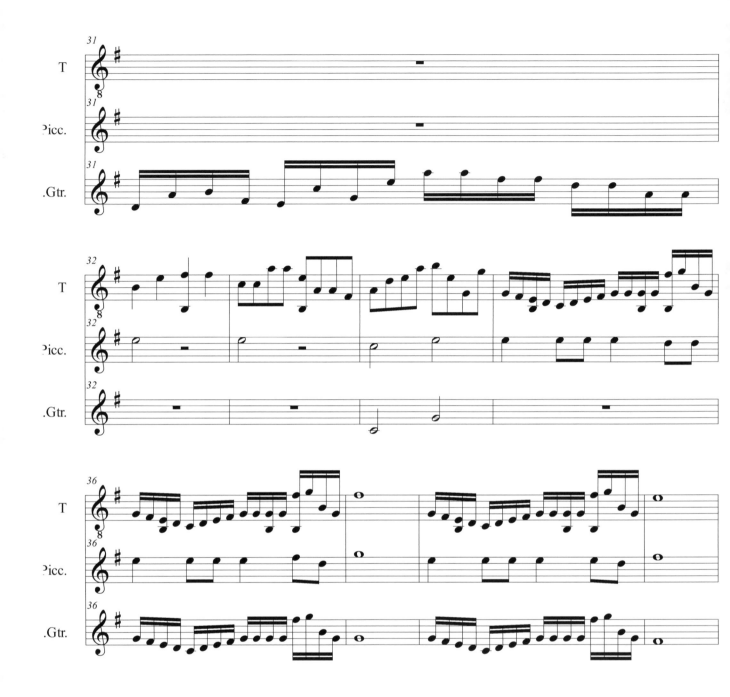

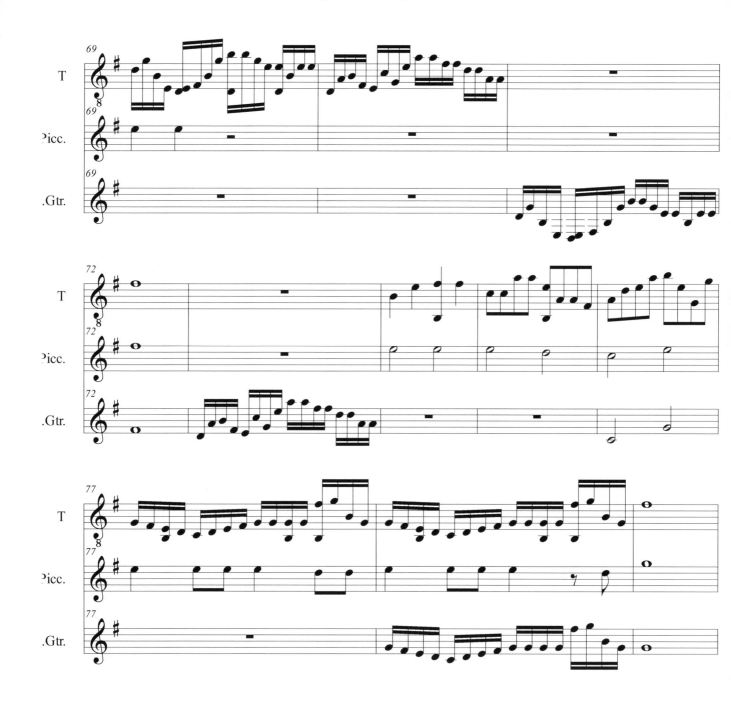

Sonata No 34, Op 281 - Sailing To Eternity - Part 2

Dr. Anis I. Milad

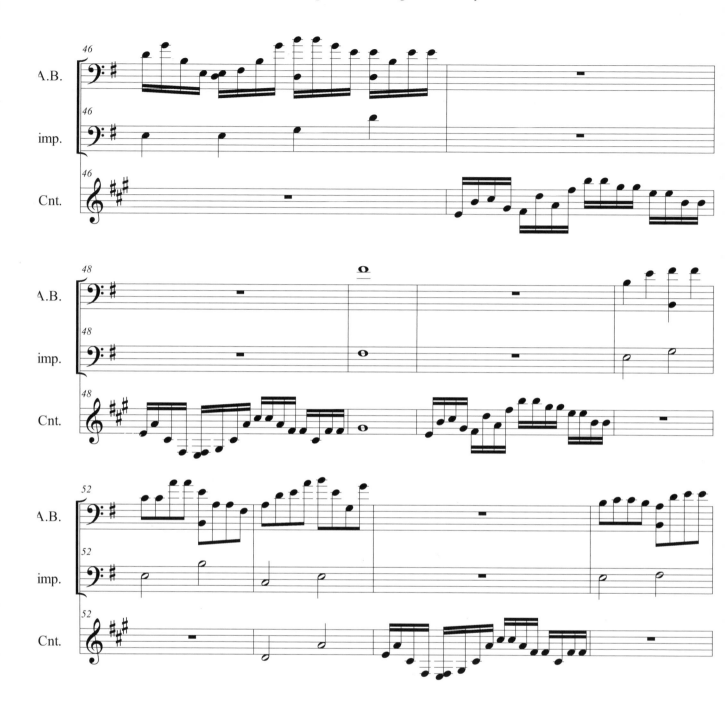

Sonata No 34, Op 281 - Sailing To Eternity - Part 2

446

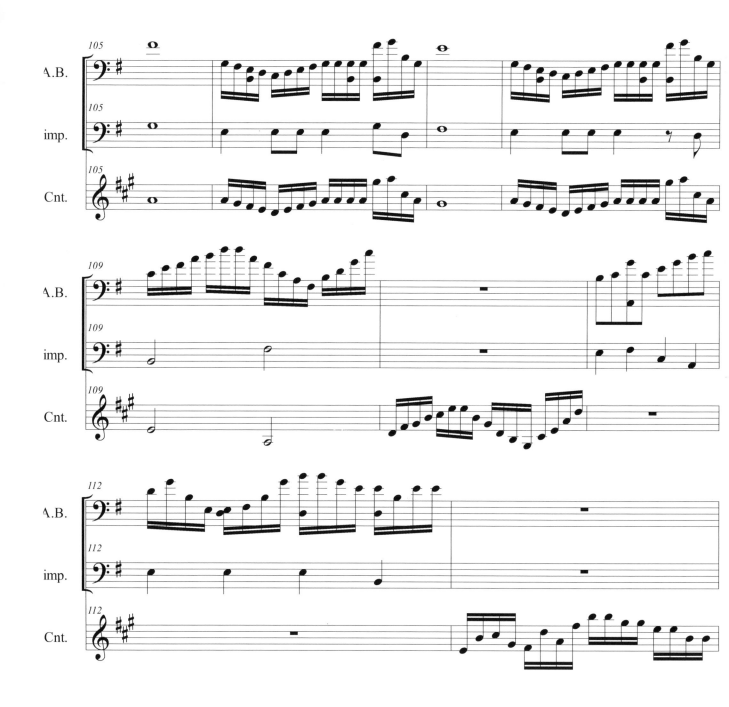

Sonata No 34, Op 281 - Sailing To Eternity - Part 3

Dr. Anis I. Milad

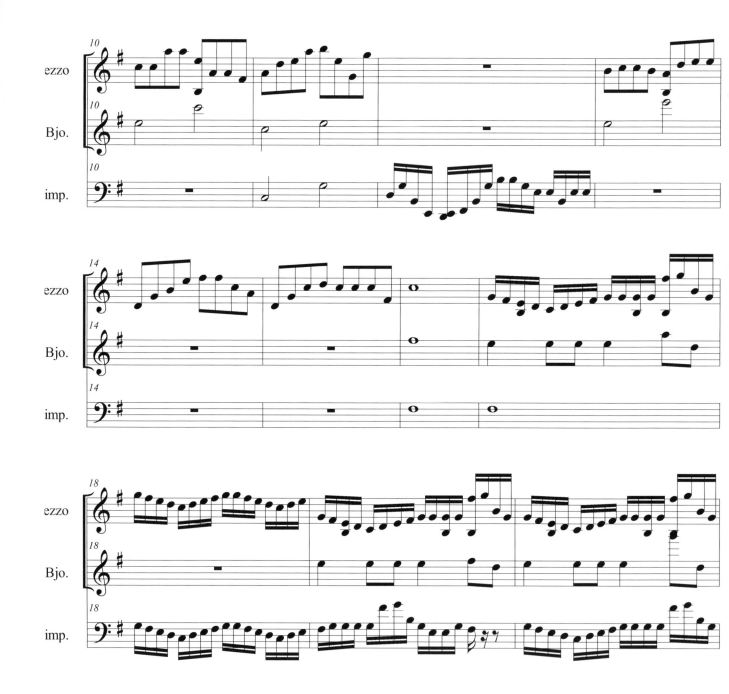

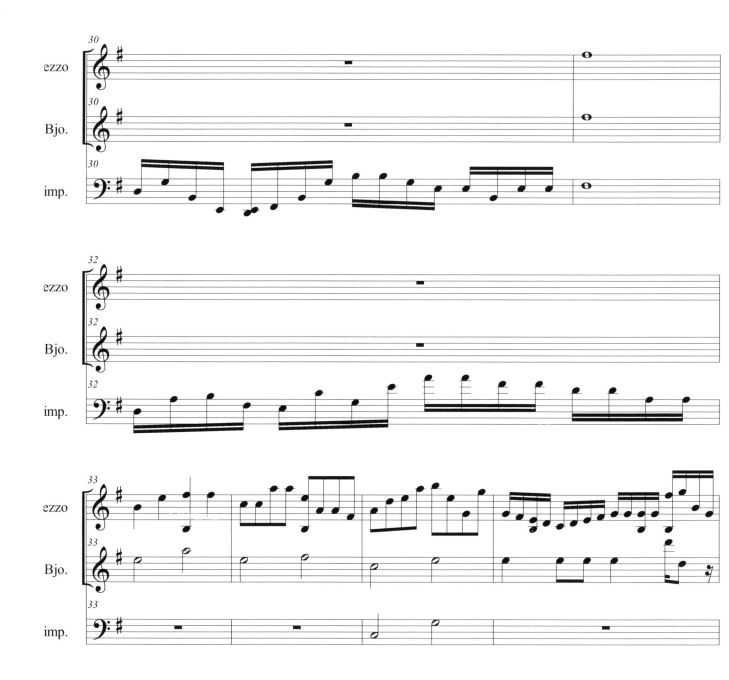

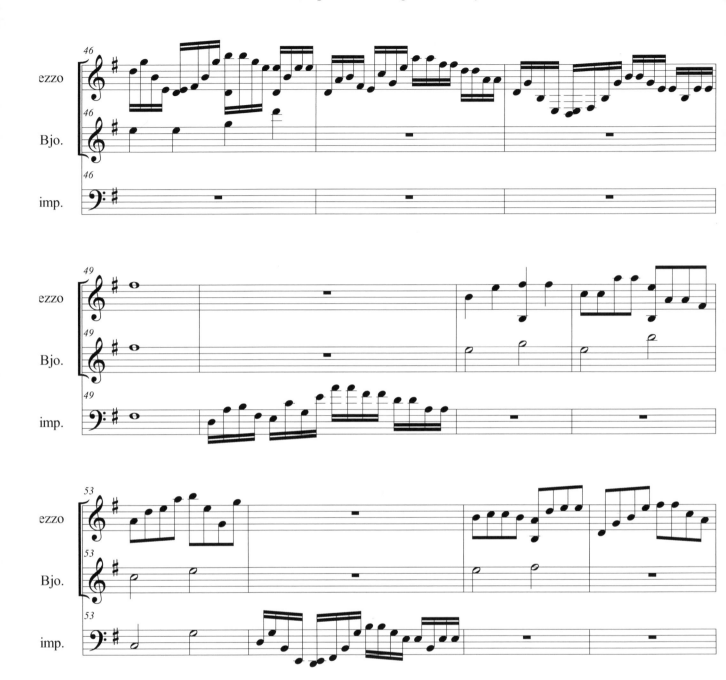

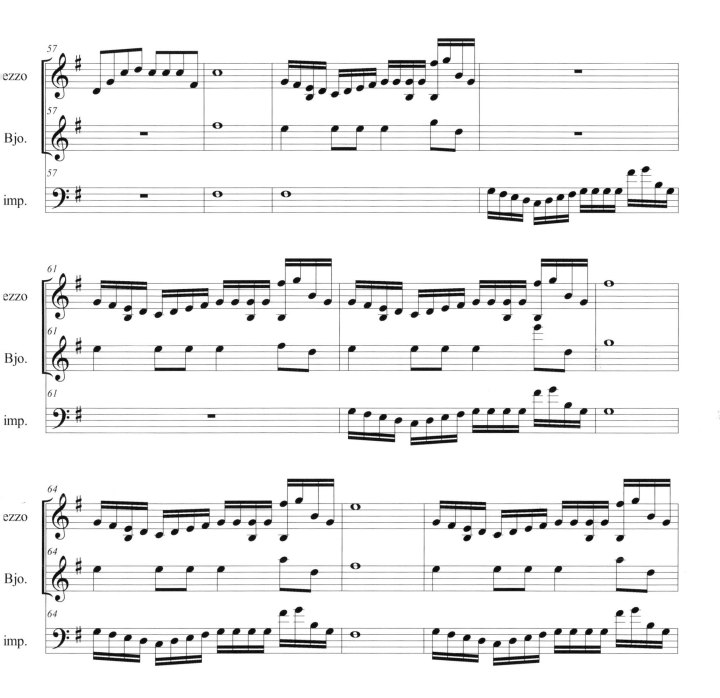

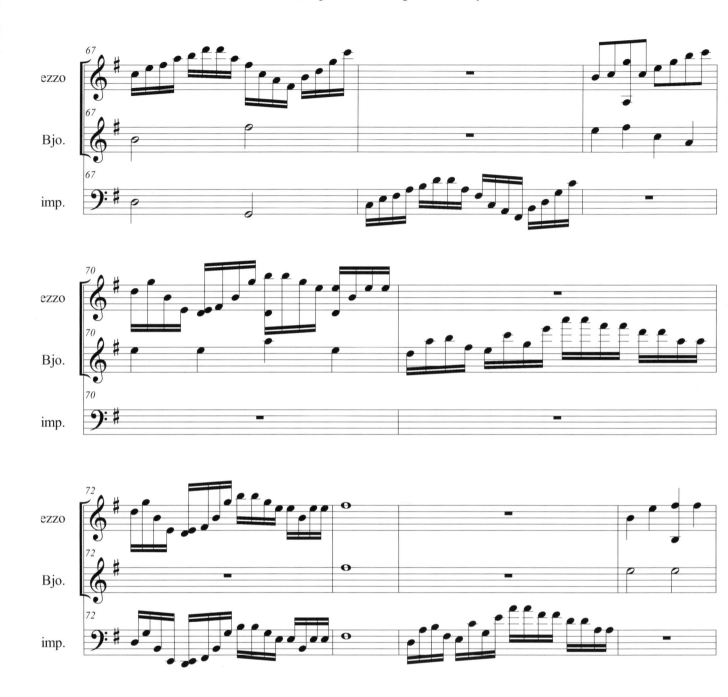

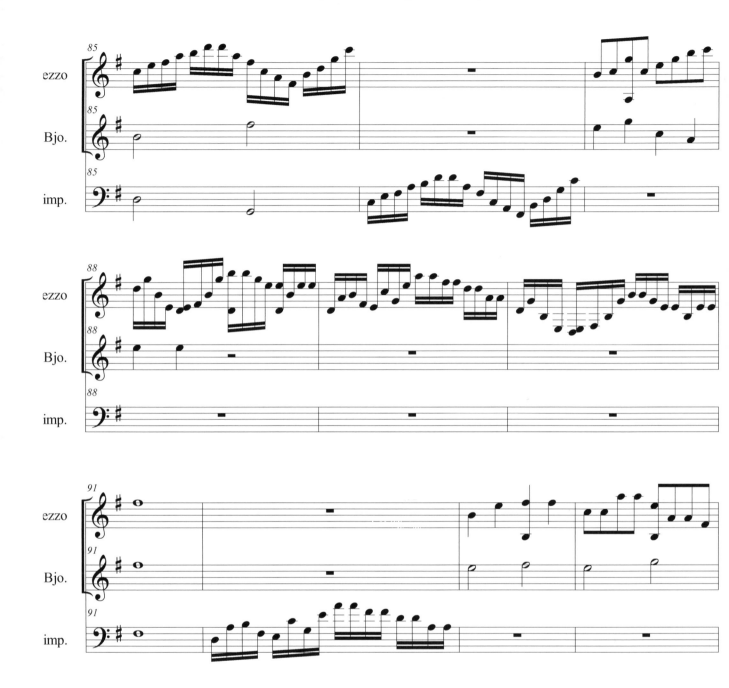